Praise for *Weeds*

"This alternative view of weeds gives a refreshing insight into some of our least popular plants."
– BBC Gardeners' World magazine

"Here is a very organic look at weeds, considering them not as invading forces to be destroyed, but as indicators of soil health, green manures, an incomparable resource for garden wildlife, compost material and even food."
– Organic Gardening

"Discover how many weeds can actually help to nurture a better, healthier and more balanced garden."
– Gardens Monthly

"Even a seasoned weed exterminator will pause and think about the design of their garden and how they might best use some of the weeds that grow there."
– The Horticulturist

"You won't find a host of chemical solutions to get rid of the weeds in your garden, but what you will find are some fascinating facts about weeds and how to deal with them naturally."
– Garden News

"A manageable length and remarkably jargon-free, this will be an extremely useful resource for any gardener."
– Pesticides News

"Rather than concentrating our efforts on preventing, clearing and controlling, we could be utilising weeds to improve the fertility of our gardens, feed our plants and encourage wildlife."
– Clean Slate

"This book remains grounded in realistic, practical gardening."
– The Organic Way

WEEDS

An organic, earth-friendly guide to their identification, use and control

John Walker
Winner of the Garden Media Guild Environmental Award

Photographs by Colin Leftley

Earth-friendly Books

For my parents

ISBN 978-0-9932683-4-2

First published in the United Kingdom in 2003 by Cassell Illustrated.

This revised edition published in the United Kingdom in 2016 by Earth-friendly Books, www.earthfriendlygardener.net

Editor: Gaby Bartai

Design: Darren Moseley at Kablooie Creative

All photographs © Colin Leftley, except for pages 9, 10, 11, 16, 18 (top), 22, 24 (bottom), 37, 42, 44, 46, 53 (bottom), 54 (top), 58 (bottom), 60 (top), 63 (top), 64 (bottom), 67 (top), 70 (top), 73 (bottom), 89, 90, 100, 102, 117 and 138 © John Walker.

Front cover: dandelion (p.60) © John Walker. Back cover insets: left, great bindweed roots among potatoes (p.84), and right, harvesting stinging nettle (p.41) © Colin Leftley; centre, bumblebee (*Bombus* sp.) foraging on a dandelion (p.10) © John Walker.

Cover design by Darren Moseley at Kablooie Creative

Disclaimer: At the time of going to press the advice and information contained in this book are believed to be true and accurate, and if edible weeds are eaten according to the guidance given here, they are safe. However, someone, somewhere, is allergic to almost anything, so if you are trying completely new weeds to eat, sample them in moderation at first. The author and publisher accept no liability for actions inspired by this book.

Contents

Welcome to the new edition

Sitting down to pen fresh words about this book, which I wrote over a decade ago, has proven both hard and easy. The world has changed in leaps and bounds; almost all of the pressures on the natural world, of which we gardeners are a part, have intensified. We are only just beginning to learn about the effects that synthetic pesticides, including weedkillers, some of which are becoming increasingly pernicious, are having on the delicate web of life around us. Residues of weedkillers sold in garden centres and supermarkets are now routinely found in our food, in our urine, and their pollution is affecting soils and aquatic ecosystems globally.

Despite all of the calls for caution, common sense somehow gets nudged aside; gardening celebrities still blithely recommend using proven-to-pollute weedkillers, and gardening publications, in thrall to big business, still accept influential advertising from the companies that manufacture them. The creep of weedkiller adverts onto television assures us that these potent poisons are a must-have to help maintain our busy-busy 'lifestyles'.

Reflecting on this resistance to change has been the hard part; actually going through the book and seeing where it might benefit from being revised has been an uplifting piece of cake. None of the organic, earth-friendly techniques I describe here need updating, because they're timeless. Filling an old inside-out compost bag with tough weeds to turn them into rich, dark compost works as well now as it did 10 years ago, and will do so decades from now. And it won't have caused a jot of pollution or harm to our natural world.

My eyes were forever opened to the wonder of weeds when I first wrote this book.

They've not closed since.

John Walker
Snowdonia, North Wales – Summer 2016

A note on how to use this book

Explanations of commonly-used gardening terms can be found in the glossary on p.118.

Throughout the book, wherever the name of an individual weed appears, it is followed by a page number, e.g. annual meadow grass (p.51). This refers to the main descriptive entry and photograph of that weed in 'Know your weeds', starting on p.49. Using these numbers you can quickly look up any weed referred to while you are reading through the book, without having to consult the full index. This should prove useful if you want to look up a weed for the first time or remind yourself what a specific weed looks like.

Foreword to the first edition

We live in a media-driven age in which we're increasingly led to believe that fast is good, that hectic is to be applauded and that we 'don't have time' for all those small things in life. Our gardening, too, has been contaminated by this frantic drive to pack more into life than is perhaps really good for us. In recent years, television makeover programmes have been widely praised for encouraging more of us to take up gardening but, for me at least, they are a double-edged sword. The idea of the 'instant' garden is a fundamentally misleading one – it just happens to work well on television. It's true, you can go out and buy all you need to quickly stick together a garden in a weekend, but creating and nurturing a garden is another matter. I'm amused – if slightly alarmed – to see a flurry of books about gardening with speed and even impatience as their central themes. You simply can't hurry gardening – or nature – along, so there's little point in being impatient with it.

One of those 'small things' in any gardener's life that remains constant is what to do about those plants that you'd rather not have growing in your flower beds, mixed borders, lawns, paths and drives or among your vegetables, herbs and fruits . These unwanted plants are, of course, what we disparagingly call 'weeds' . The modern quick fix for dealing with weeds is to use chemical weedkillers (herbicides). It's certainly a tempting solution: all you need do is apply them to the weeds and they shrivel and die. I've used weedkillers myself in the past and have seen how apparently 'effective' some of them are.

All around us, evidence that we are damaging our environment continues to mount. We now talk glibly of the 'greenhouse effect' as if it were just part and parcel of everyday life, rather than a serious threat to the earth's future. But what, you must be thinking, has any of this got to do with weeds? Well, I believe that our gardens are the perfect and most natural places to begin doing our bit both to ease the strain we are putting on the earth and to reverse some of the damage already done – hence this is an earth-friendly guide to tackling weeds.

Stinging nettles twist and buckle after being sprayed with weedkiller

Organic gardening is all about working with, rather than against, nature. Uprooting a weed, rather than spraying it with some synthetic chemical weedkiller, might not strike you as a profound gesture we gardeners can make to 'save the planet', but imagine if hundreds, thousands or millions of gardeners did it: that's an awful lot of weeds and a mighty amount of weedkiller staying put in its bottle. So this isn't a book full of lists of weeds and which chemical to put on them. In fact, it isn't solely about getting rid of weeds, although identification of some of the commonest garden weeds and how to deal with them make up the largest section of the book. In part, you could see it as a celebration of weeds.

I hope that this book will show you weeds in a new light, encourage you to think about them differently, and, perhaps most importantly, help you deal gently yet effectively with those weeds you don't want, in a way that is kind to the earth. It might also – dare I say it – actually persuade you to leave some weeds well alone, or even encourage them in your garden.

John Walker – Spring 2003

Introduction

As ideas for this book first began to germinate in my mind, I spent many hours gazing out onto a patchwork of narrow gardens some 30m (100ft) long and 3m (10ft) wide, my own included. Now, in spring, every garden I can see has at least some weeds in it. The most neglected and abandoned strips are smothered in the first flush of bright yellow dandelion flowers and the air above them is buzzing with insect life, from tattered butterflies coming out of hibernation to bees of all shapes and sizes seeking out the first prized nectar of spring.

My own garden is three-quarters covered with a weed-suppressing mulch and some carefully laid old carpet (which just happens to be green!). This is to see off a dense thicket of couch grass, which has colonised a large area. In a year's time I'll be able to roll it back, fork out any persistent remnants of the couch and plant straight into the rich, black soil. The gentle passing of time will help me eradicate these tenacious weeds.

A bumblebee feasts on an early dandelion flower

Stinging nettle shoot tips make a tasty soup

At the end of my garden shed the first shoots of the perennial stinging nettle are pushing up from between my water butts. Its tough, spreading underground stems are easily contained by the bricks of the shed base and it's growing in a spot which would otherwise be unused. The tender young shoot tips will make a tasty and nutritious soup; then, later in the summer, I'll cut the leafy mineral-rich shoots and either add them to the compost heap or dunk them in a bucket to make a wonderful liquid plant food. Part of the patch will be left to grow tall and flower, providing a food source for the hungry caterpillars of small tortoiseshell, peacock and red admiral butterflies. Frogs, ground beetles and other beneficial creatures find the dense jungle of nettle stems an ideal place from which to launch their nightly forays in search of slugs. Should the nettles stray from their allotted patch, it'll be a simple enough job to cut the shoots low to the ground and bury them under a deep mulch of straw or hay.

Just over the road, on my allotment, tiny forests of seedlings are appearing on patches of bare soil, with self-sown pot marigolds (*Calendula*), borage and opium poppy among them. My Dutch hoe, brought to razor sharpness, will see off any unwanted weed seedlings in a flash, but I'll be sparing some of the pot marigolds and borage to attract beneficial insects during the summer. I'll also be picking their flowers to scatter on summer salads; then, later on, I'll gather the poppy seeds to sprinkle on home-made bread.

Season-to-month conversion chart

I have used general seasonal terms as broadly applicable to the English Midlands. References to season can be equated with specific months as follows:

Early spring	March
Mid-spring	April
Late spring	May
Early summer	June
Mid-summer	July
Late summer	August
Early autumn	September
Mid-autumn	October
Late autumn	November
Early winter	December
Mid-winter	January
Late winter	February

1.

WEEDS
One of nature's success stories

Weeds are amazing. When I stumble upon a clump of creeping thistle (p.59), its pink, honey-scented flowers smothered with butterflies, bees and hoverflies during summer, I can't help but stop and feel humbled. But when I find its prickly shoots pushing up between my potatoes, and carefully try to loosen the soil so I can gently tease out its fleshy roots, I'm both irritated and amazed at the same time. Irritated that this tough perennial weed hasn't yet been eradicated from my vegetable beds – and amazed that I thought it could be. Any plant that can send its roots deep into the soil and is able to grow into a whole new plant from the tiniest root fragment is, you have to admit, pretty amazing.

What is a weed?

Pushing up among my potatoes is the last place I want creeping thistle to be growing, but just down the road, on a bare plot destined for building, there is a massive clump where some of the stems, at over 2m (6ft), are taller than I am. Here this beautiful wild plant seems perfectly at home, as it truly is when growing along hedgerows and banks everywhere. In my vegetable beds, creeping thistle is a serious weed problem, while on wild, uncultivated ground it is growing where it 'should' be. As soon as any plant, wild or cultivated, begins growing where we don't want it – in the 'wrong' place – it becomes a weed.

One of the most serious of all weeds, Japanese knotweed (p.68), was first introduced to this country in 1825 as an outstanding and much-heralded garden plant. Today its spread is so serious that at least one local authority employs someone whose job is solely concerned with its eradication! This is just one of several plants that started out being grown in the 'right' place, but which over time have become notorious for growing where we really don't want them. Japanese knotweed is one of the most amazing, useful and resilient weeds I know, yet it is also one of

Pushing up through a path, both this raspberry sucker and the great bindweed entwining it are weeds

the most pernicious. You might be cursing me at this point if you have it in your garden, but despite all its bad press and the fact that it can be an offence to grow or spread it, I feel it deserves a second look – see p.23.

So weeds are, by definition, simply any plants growing where we don't want them. This applies across the board. Even a walnut sapling in the middle of my vegetable patch, sprouting from a mislaid nut buried by a squirrel the previous autumn, is a weed, just as much as great bindweed (p.63) is, with its stranglehold on the plants in your herbaceous border.

The 'healing' role of weeds

Bare, exposed soil isn't part of nature's master plan. How many examples can you think of where soil is naturally found bare and with no plants at all growing in it? Good examples are beneath freshly uprooted trees, landslips, or where the ground has been charred following a heathland fire. In these situations bare soil isn't bare for long; within days seedlings begin to appear and cover the ground with a miniature green forest. In a few months' time the scar is barely noticeable. A year later you would never know it had been there at all.

Contrast these natural examples of bare soil with those created by man: ploughed fields and freshly dug gardens and allotments are obvious examples. But, left to nature, even these vast expanses of bare soil soon turn green with a multitude of tiny seedlings. Think of those wild, overgrown allotments or that jungle-like abandoned garden – these too were once bare earth. In fields, gardens and allotments, on lawns, roadside verges and sports fields, along streets and on paths and pavements, we are constantly battling to stop weeds from growing. All we are doing is keeping the healing powers of nature at bay.

Weeds act like a kind of living 'plaster' whenever soil is exposed, either by natural or artificial causes. As far as nature goes, bare soil is out. When soil is exposed to sunlight it's not only the earthworms that quickly burrow back into the darkness. Millions of microscopic soil organisms are also exposed to the potentially harmful rays of the sun, so the sooner plant growth covers the soil over again, the better. Once you appreciate this perfectly natural reaction by nature, you start to see that weeds aren't there to deliberately frustrate our gardening efforts; they are simply doing their job. Just as new skin forms after we've caught ourselves on a rose thorn, weeds help heal wounds in the earth. Look at it another way: it's us who are causing the problem by insisting on bare, neat-looking soil – open wounds, if you like.

Self-seeded forget-me-nots (Myosotis spp.) soon start to colonise disturbed ground. In a few weeks there will be no bare soil

This abandoned building plot is being reclaimed by pioneering weeds

Fertility builders

Left to their own devices, weeds also help to improve the fertility of the soil. They do this in several ways. Their roots bind the soil together, helping to improve its structure and create a more stable environment in which soil life can flourish. Those weeds with a deep taproot, such as curled dock (p.59), draw up plant nutrients from deeper in the ground, making them available to plants growing near the soil surface. Above ground, the stems of weeds help trap fallen leaves and other organic matter, which break down into the soil or are dragged underground by earthworms. And when the weeds themselves finally die – after weeks, months or years depending on the type of weed and its life cycle (see p.25) – both the leafy tops and the roots decompose into valuable humus.

As the soil becomes more and more fertile, different kinds of plants start to replace the 'pioneering' weeds. In the UK a typical succession might see shrubs moving in to oust the pioneers by gradually shading them out, followed in turn by trees, which eventually push up through the shrubs, finally shading them out too. The leaves that fall from the shrubs and trees carry on the job of building soil fertility that was begun by those very first weeds that sprang up on the bare soil. Then, when one of these mature trees is uprooted in a storm, ripping open a wound of bare soil in the earth, the whole process starts again.

Of course, in our gardens and allotments we buck this natural route to fertility by actively discouraging weeds and adding our own goodness in the form of garden compost, manure or natural fertilisers. This isn't to say that certain weeds, such as perennial stinging nettle (p.78), cannot be used as part of the overall fertility-building plan for your garden, as we will discover later in this book. In fact, virtually all weeds, even the most pernicious, like great bindweed (p.63), can be put to good use. For me, working with weeds, realising then releasing their potential, is one of the basic tenets of an organic approach.

What do weeds tell us?

Probably the single most important thing you can do, when you take on a neglected and overgrown garden or allotment, is nothing – at least to begin with. Studying the existing weed cover, especially during spring and summer, can tell you a lot about the kind of soil and the growing conditions you will find as you bring the garden or allotment under control. 'Reading' your garden in this way is obviously going to be more difficult during the autumn and winter, when weed growth has died down, but if you really can't resist getting stuck in and starting to clear overgrown areas, you can still look out for tell-tale signs of perennials, whose dormant underground parts will be obvious when you dig or fork the soil.

Letting weeds grow on a bare patch of soil will give you an insight into the condition of your soil and help you learn to identify them as seedlings

See what comes up

One way of getting to know both your weeds and the type, the level of fertility and the pH (acidity or alkalinity) of your soil is to clear an area and wait to see what appears. Encouraging weeds like this might seem an open invitation for trouble, but if you clear an area of around 1sq m (1sq yd), it's easy enough to pull up most maturing weeds before they start to spread seeds. If you try this, you aren't waiting for weed seeds

Borage seedlings have bright green, bristly leaves, making them easy to spot

to invade this experimental patch, but simply encouraging the dormant weed seeds already in the soil to spring into life (poppy seeds can lie dormant in the soil for up to 100 years). You might be surprised at what grows. Try to check the patch regularly – daily if possible – as your soil gives up its 'secrets', so that you can learn to identify plants from the very early stages of growth, right up until they flower. This knowledge will help you in future when, for example, you're hoeing seedling weeds. If you know what pot marigolds (p.73), borage (p.53) and opium poppies (p.72) look like when just a few weeks old, it's easier to spare some.

A good sign: sun spurge indicates a fertile soil rich in plant nutrients

Hidden riches: clumps of perennial stinging nettles are a sure indicator of fertile soil, so think positive if you find them in a new garden and don't be in a rush to chop them down – they won't sting unless you touch them. Nettles thrive on the sites of old bonfires, near heaps of animal manure and near or, as seen here, actually in compost bins. These nettles aren't doing any harm (apart from the odd sting) and can be cut regularly, then added to the top of the bin, where they both help with breakdown of organic matter and add valuable plant nutrients, such as nitrogen and iron. When the bin is emptied it's an easy job to fork out the yellow nettle roots. Read more about this amazingly versatile weed on p.41

The great majority of weeds tend, like most garden plants, to do well in a slightly acid to neutral soil – one with a pH of 6.5–7.0 – while others only thrive in very specific soil conditions and are often called 'indicator' weeds. These give us clues to what type of soil we have, as well as to factors such as how well or badly drained it is, or how the ground might have been treated in the past. If you find sheep's sorrel (p.76) on your plot, the soil will be quite acid; creeping buttercup (p.58) thrives in moist, poorly-drained soil, while patches of pineapple weed (p.73) indicate hard, well-trodden ground. The presence of some weeds is a good sign: chickweed (p.56), borage (p.53), redshank (p.74) and sun spurge (p.78) are all signs of a fertile soil. Weeds like these can cause you future headaches, because as you get your garden into shape and start to boost soil fertility they are ready and waiting to move in.

But there are other ways to interpret the weed cover you find in a new garden. If you've just taken on a brand new house, the chances are that, come spring, your garden will be home to mainly 'pioneer' weeds – those that have been waiting patiently as dormant seeds, and have now made the most of being exposed to the sunlight. Any bare soil is likely to be covered with a green carpet of weeds, as nature begins to take over. In a brand new garden like this, soil fertility could be quite low, especially if the more fertile top 30–45cm (12–18in) of topsoil has been mixed with less fertile subsoil from below this depth, during building work. If very few weeds appear, it could indicate that mostly subsoil has been spread over your garden, meaning you have plenty of work to do on soil improvement.

At the other extreme, an older, overgrown garden might be swamped by thickets of bramble (p.54) or creeping thistle (p.59) as well as cultivated plants gone wild. Here soil fertility is likely to be surprisingly high once the ground is cleared and you start growing the plants you want. It might be hard work removing tough, perennial weeds, but in a long-neglected garden, nature has been busily but quietly improving the fertility of the soil – so make the most of it.

Wildlife and weeds

One of my favourite country walks cuts right through a large field, which most summers grows a crop of cereals, either barley or wheat. Like the vast majority of agricultural land used for cereal production, the crop is sprayed regularly with synthetic chemicals (pesticides, fungicides and herbicides) to control pests, diseases – and weeds. At the start of the path, the hedgerows and wildflower-rich field margins are alive with the buzz of countless insects going about their business. You really can hear the life around you. As well as the insects, small mammals scuffle along the hedge bottoms and birds flit through the undergrowth.

One day, in high summer, it struck me just how denuded of wildlife the centre of the field actually was. Yes, you could hear the song thrush in the distance, but the air carried no more than the occasional passing insect and, looking down, there were only the regimented rows of cereal as far as the eye could see. There were no wild plants – weeds – to be seen, apart from a few wild grasses cowering beneath the corn; they'd long ago succumbed to the farmer's merciless weedkiller. Leaving the field on the other side, I walked back into a frenzy of wild, teeming life. It was like stepping back into another world.

The author among a dense clump of creeping thistle, a valuable food source for butterflies and bees, which is often found on rough ground

Some gardens and allotments are like the centre of that field. They might look neat, tidy and well-kept, but when you look closer, the air is empty of insects, there might be fewer birds around and wildlife in general is very much at a premium. Of course it's true that you can grow cultivated 'garden' plants to attract wildlife, especially insects, into your garden, but it's the naturally occurring weeds growing wild and free that really make the difference. This is because they have always been there. It's their patch – they've evolved and adapted over time to make the best of the specific growing conditions around them. Wild animals and insects have evolved alongside them and they depend on each other. That's why that field is so quiet and barren of wildlife in the centre: all the weeds have gone and so have the creatures that rely on them.

A dramatic decline in the numbers of some of our best-loved wild birds is now well-documented. As well as the more obvious factors, such as the destruction of their natural habitats, other less obvious factors are at work, such as a reduction in available food for birds (and other wild animals). If there are fewer wild plants – which in that field become weeds as soon as they appear among the corn – it stands to reason that there are fewer insects feeding and breeding on them, so there is less food for insect-eating birds. Therefore, by eliminating weeds, we reduce insect numbers, the birds have less to eat and so their populations decline.

The same goes for seed-eating birds, such as goldfinches – if we wipe out all the teasels (p.79), we deprive them of a valuable food source and ourselves of the joy of watching them on a winter's day. If this seems rather too simplistic an explanation, however, that's because it is. The interrelationships between all living things are much more complex; insects rely on plants – weeds – for food and shelter, just as much as the plants rely on the insects to bring about pollination and fertilisation of their flowers and, with some, dispersal of the resulting seeds.

It's easy to begin to see just what a vital role wild plants, or weeds (whichever cap fits), play – not only in the overall ecology of the natural world, but also in your own garden's 'ecosystem'. In many areas, wild 'weeds' have been banished by weedkillers to field margins, where they often cling to a somewhat precarious existence. To search out weeds to photograph for this book, I didn't head for the countryside, but walked the streets of my town. It was here that I came across the greatest variety of weeds. Yes, I did see many gardens and allotments with not a weed in sight, but I also came across wild, overgrown gardens and forgotten corners, filled with weeds – and life.

Intensive farming has banished many weeds to the edges of fields

Friend and foe?

I paid a massive clump of Japanese knotweed (p.68) a visit whilst writing this book. Pushing into its forest of stems, which were 2.5m (8ft) tall or more, I stepped into another world. I was surrounded by the buzz of insects feeding on its nectar-rich flowers, while below me was a carpet of brown, hollow stems, with spiders and other insects scurrying over them. I was once served some young, cooked shoots of this weed, which look similar to asparagus. They had a pleasant, slightly acidic flavour and were certainly a talking point. The young shoots are also a good substitute for rhubarb in jam and pies.

Japanese knotweed forms large, dense clumps

So far so good, but what if I told you I had seen this plant bursting up through tarmac and concrete, that its tough underground rhizomes can penetrate 2m (6ft) or more deep into the ground, or that there are reports of it sending rhizomes underneath a motorway? Would you want it near your garden? But consider this. In some areas, where Japanese knotweed has been studied closely, it's been found that these plants are creating a valuable habitat for a wide range of creatures, including insects, spiders, frogs and grass snakes. It seems that insects in particular like to overwinter in the hollow stems, leading to an increase in the frog population, followed by that of the grass snakes which feed on the frogs.

Beneath the current year's shoots is a dense mat of old, hollow stems, which are used by overwintering insects

While it can be an offence, in certain areas, to grow, plant or spread Japanese knotweed in the wild, this does illustrate that no weed is entirely without its good points. Any plant which can offer so many positive attributes surely deserves our respect rather than our derision.

Killed by weedkiller, these tough dry Japanese knotweed stems are helping another weed – great bindweed (p.63) – to thrive

2.

SECRETS OF SUCCESS
How weeds grow and spread

To appreciate weeds and deal with them effectively – and organically – you need to know how they tick. Each weed in your garden is programmed to grow, spread and survive in its own unique way. Understanding the survival strategies of weeds lies at the heart of earth-friendly weed control. Groundsel (p.65) lives a fleeting existence, with a life span, from seed to mature, seed-bearing plant, of just a few weeks, and can be dealt with by a single pass of a sharp hoe. Bramble (p.54), on the other hand, can form a dense, woody thicket that marches on relentlessly for decades and often requires superhuman effort to remove it. Knowing how weeds live out their lives – what their 'life cycles' are – is the first step to eradicating those you don't want.

Weed life cycles

A 'life cycle' is simply a way of describing how any weed grows to maturity and over what timescale. Once you become familiar with each type of life cycle, you can judge when the most effective time is to tackle that weed. For virtually all weeds, the single most effective time to control them is when they are small seedlings. At this stage in any weed's life cycle, it's a simple case of hoeing the young plants off (see p.104). But wait a month or two and things are very different. It will still be possible to hoe off shallow-rooted weeds, but others will have sent roots deep into the soil and, if you hoe these off, they'll simply shoot up again from below the ground. Wait six months and it'll be almost impossible to use a hoe as the ground will be covered in a dense carpet of weeds.

• **Annual weeds** – these germinate, grow, flower, produce seeds and die all within a single year. Some, like chickweed (p.56), can produce several successive generations within a single year and are sometimes called ephemeral weeds. Annuals are a problem on ground that is disturbed and cultivated regularly, such as the vegetable garden, but if you adopt a no-dig approach (see p.100) and use mulches (see p.92), their numbers can be drastically reduced.

• **Biennial weeds** – during the first year these germinate and grow, producing a clump or rosette of leaves, and often a thick underground root, which lies dormant during the winter. The following year, the plant produces flowers, sets seeds and then dies. You're more likely to find biennials, such as teasel (p.79), in borders and among permanent plants, where the soil is less disturbed. Like annuals, biennials can be reduced through a no-dig approach and by using mulches.

• **Perennial weeds** – once established these grow indefinitely, often for many years, and can make huge, spreading plants – Japanese knotweed (p.68; see also p.23) is a good example. They survive from year to year in a number of ways, such as, in the case of dandelion (p.60), dormant roots. Perennial weeds may still flower and produce seeds each year, but they can also spread rapidly in other ways. Although perennial weeds are usually more of a problem in gardens that have been left untended for some time, they can quickly establish on bare soil, while the spreading underground parts of some, such as great bindweed (p.63), can quickly invade from a neighbour's weedy plot.

These life cycle categories are useful in helping us to understand more about weeds, but they can sometimes still confound us. On my allotment it's not unusual to find young plants of opium poppy (p.72), borage (p.53) and nipplewort (p.71) looking green and healthy in the middle of winter. If the weather stays mild, these young plants will race ahead in spring and produce the earliest flowers, but a severe freeze will kill them outright. All of these weeds are more usually thought of as annuals, but in this case they act more like biennials. This is just one example of how weeds, like other plants, sometimes break the rules.

Common weeds by life cycle

Numbers refer to the page number for each main weed entry – see 'Know your weeds', p.49.

Annuals:

Annual meadow grass (p.51)
Black medick (p.52)
Black nightshade (p.52)
Borage* (p.53)
California poppy (p.54)
Canadian fleabane (p.55)
Chickweed* (p.56)
Cleavers (p.56)
Common field speedwell (p.57)
Fat hen (p.61)
Groundsel* (p.65)
Hairy bittercress* (p.65)
Himalayan balsam (p.66)

Knotgrass (p.69)
Love-in-a-mist (p.71)
Nipplewort (p.71)
Opium poppy (p.72)
Pineapple weed (p.73)
Pot marigold (p.73)
Redshank (p.74)
Scarlet pimpernel (p.75)
Shepherd's purse* (p.77)
Smooth sow thistle (p.77)
Sun spurge (p.78)
Yellow oxalis (p.80)
(*Ephemerals)

Biennials:

Evening primrose (p.61)
Giant hogweed (p.63)
Hogweed (p.67)
Hollyhock (p.67)

Honesty (p.68)
Land cress (p.70)
Ragwort (p.74)
Teasel (p.79)

Perennials:

Bird's-foot trefoil (p.51)
Bracken (p.53)
Bramble (p.54)
Canadian golden-rod (p.55)
Coltsfoot (p.57)
Couch grass (p.58)
Creeping buttercup (p.58)
Creeping thistle (p.59)
Curled dock (p.59)
Daisy (p.60)
Dandelion (p.60)
Field bindweed (p.62)
Field horsetail (p.62)
Great bindweed (p.63)

Great willow herb (p.64)
Ground elder (p.64)
Hoary plantain (p.66)
Japanese knotweed (p.68)
Lady's mantle (p.69)
Lesser hawkbit (p.70)
Pearlwort (p.72)
Rosebay willow herb (p.75)
Self-heal (p.76)
Sheep's sorrel (p.76)
Stinging nettle (p.78)
White clover (p.79)
Yarrow (p.80)

Getting around – how weeds spread

In late summer, while writing this part of the book, I decided to go and track down some weeds on a previously cultivated allotment, which had been left to its own devices since the spring. Pushing through the thick green carpet – there was no bare soil – was a revelation. The small, lightweight seeds of groundsel (p.65) and smooth sow thistle (p.77), each with its own tiny 'parachute', took to the air, while overhead, clouds of creeping thistle (p.59) and rosebay willow herb (p.75) seeds floated past on the breeze, launched from unseen plants on the other side of a fence. Brushing past an opium poppy (p.72) sent thousands of tiny seeds showering to the ground, shaken from their dry, pepperpot-like seed-heads. In the cracks along the path, diminutive pearlwort (p.72) offered up its tiny pods of dust-like seeds to the slightest breeze. Nearby, the offspring of a patch of self-sown borage (p.53) engulfed courgettes, planted in a last-ditch attempt at growing some fresh vegetables. A makeshift greenhouse had been invaded by great bindweed (p.63), its creeping roots having slid quietly under the wooden frame, while not far away a spreading mat of field bindweed (p.62) was alive with a frenzy of insects popping in and out of its pink, scented trumpets. Moist soil around a leaking water butt had become the perfect home for a dense colony of creeping buttercup (p.58), which was sending out runners to conquer the rest of the plot.

The tiny, airborne seeds of creeping thistle are embedded in dense, fluffy down

Inside this makeshift greenhouse, great bindweed is in flower weeks ahead of plants growing outdoors

Just by walking around this allotment I had the chance not only to marvel at the simple yet ingenious ways in which weeds spread, but also to take part in their dispersal. Unseen hairy bittercress (p.65) and pearlwort (p.72) seeds were doubtless embedded in the soil on my boots, while the large, round, sticky seeds of cleavers (p.56) and probably a few groundsel (p.65) and smooth sow thistle (p.77) clung to my socks. These weeds could then have travelled anything from a few feet to several, if not hundreds of, miles. Those weeds that rely on seeds for their spread and survival do so in a variety of different ways.

Each brown dandelion seed is attached to a silky 'parachute'

Taking to the air

To get into the air and then be carried by its currents, seeds need to be light and also to have some means of catching in the wind. Once up and away, airborne seeds can be carried over great distances, sometimes high up in the atmosphere. Dandelion (p.60) is a familiar example of a weed which disperses its seeds by air. Each seed is attached to the end of a parachute-like structure which allows it to be carried along on the breeze. Weeds with airborne seeds can trigger over-the-fence arguments between neighbours or allotment holders; during the growing season an overgrown plot is a source of thousands of mobile seeds. Other examples include creeping thistle (p.59), great and rosebay willow herb (p.75) and groundsel (p.65).

Explosive tendencies

When the narrow pods of hairy bittercress (p.65) explode, they fling their seeds for up to 90cm (3ft) in all directions and you can hear a faint 'pop' as they go off. When the offspring of this first explosive episode produce their seeds (in what can be just a few weeks) they in turn spread their seeds the same distance. No wonder then that this has become one of our most widespread and troublesome garden weeds. But the real secret of its success is that both plants and seeds are often found in the tops of plant pots. Just a single plant, unwittingly brought back from the garden centre, could lead to hairy bittercress invading, in time, every corner of your garden! Another example is Himalayan balsam (p.66; also see p.30).

Far and wide

In early autumn, clumps of Himalayan balsam (p.66) fill the air with the scent of ripening plums, but be careful if you go in close to sniff the flowers – the seed pods of this remarkable weed explode when touched, with force enough to make your face smart! In fact the pods, which suddenly wind up like coils when triggered, are capable of firing the large seeds up to 5m (16ft) from the parent plant. This annual prefers to grow in damp soil, along streams and rivers, where the ripe seeds are also carried along by the water. Little wonder then that this is one of the fastest-spreading introduced weeds in the UK. Despite its reputation for choking some waterways, there is a flip side. Insects – bumblebees in particular – find the nectar-rich flowers irresistible and it is unquestionably a beautiful plant, although it has now been banned from some of our major flower shows in an attempt to check its relentless spread.

The ripe seed pods scatter the large dark seeds over several metres/yards

Hitching a ride

Look closely at the seeds of cleavers (p.56) and you'll see they are covered in tiny barbed hooks – as is the whole plant – which catch in clothing and animal fur. When the seeds are picked or groomed out, they fall to the ground, all ready to germinate and grow into new plants. As well as having explosive pods, the seeds of hairy bittercress (p.65) become sticky when wet, allowing them to hitch a ride on the soil clinging to your boots. The seeds of bramble (p.54) 'travel' inside birds and animals, including ourselves, then pass out later on.

Check your socks for the hitch-hiking seeds of cleavers

Other seed survival strategies

Weeds also utilise sheer strength of numbers, time and self-reliance to ensure their survival.

Strength in numbers

It has been estimated that just one cubic foot (28 litres) of soil can contain as many as 5,000 individual weed seeds. Although staggering, this becomes more believable when you realise that a single plant of smooth sow thistle (p.77), an annual weed, can produce up to 25,000 seeds during its life. A single plant of another prolific seeder, rosebay willow herb (p.75), can produce 80,000 seeds, each one capable of being carried on the wind. This 'seed bank' is constantly being topped up as new weeds grow and add to it.

Lying in wait

Although many weeds produce huge amounts of seed, even the most prolific also keep their options open. Some seeds do fall to the ground and germinate almost straight away, when conditions are ideal, but others become buried deeper in the soil, where they become dormant, waiting for their chance. It can be a long wait: knotgrass (p.69) seeds can lie low for 60 years, those of opium poppy (p.72) for around 100. It's a sobering thought that there are weed seeds hidden in the soil which are probably older than you are. What keeps most weed seeds dormant is lack of sunlight, which is why a no-dig approach (see p.100) and the use of mulches (see p.92) are so effective, especially in earth-friendly weed control. As well as light, temperature is important in triggering the germination of some weeds. While annual meadow grass (p.51) germinates, grows and produces seeds virtually year-round, including during winter, many weeds wait for the warmth of spring. Others, such as chickweed (p.56), won't germinate during a heatwave.

No insects, no problem

Some canny weeds have developed foolproof techniques to produce seeds, come what may. Most flowering weeds rely on insects and other creatures to transfer their pollen between flowers, which is known as pollination. If this is followed by successful fertilisation, seeds are produced. Dandelion (p.60), however, has done away with reliance on insects and can produce

Each pepperpot-like seed-head of opium poppy contains thousands of seeds, which rattle when ripe. They can lie dormant for 100 years

viable seeds without pollination or fertilisation (which is known as apomixis), although this doesn't stop it being a valuable source of nectar for insects during spring and early summer. The flowers of shepherd's purse (p.77) are self-fertilising, meaning that just a single plant on its own is capable of effective reproduction.

How weeds spread vegetatively

Weeds that survive from generation to generation as seed are both planning for the future and keeping their options open. The great bindweed (p.63) weaving its roots through my potatoes is going all out to ensure its survival right now. Many perennial weeds spread by what are known as 'vegetative' methods. This simply means that they grow larger and colonise fresh ground by extending the reach of their roots, rhizomes, stolons,

These wiry roots of field bindweed go deep into the soil, but can also spread sideways

runners or bulbs, while many also spread by seed as well. It's these weeds that are usually the most challenging of all.

Roots, rhizomes and bulbs can become almost invisible during the winter months, when the leaves and shoots of many weeds have died away. If you take on a garden in winter, it might at first appear to be free of weeds, but some of the most persistent perennials could be lying dormant below the surface. It's always worth looking out for any tell-tale signs: dead, stringy stems of great bindweed (p.63) woven through a hedge, mats of brown, wiry field bindweed (p.62) stems disappearing into the soil on an allotment, or the prickly brown remnants of creeping thistle (p.59).

There are various ways in which weeds spread using vegetative means:

Roots

As well as having deep taproots, both creeping thistle (p.59) and field bindweed (p.62) send out spreading lateral roots in all directions. Where these break the surface of the soil, new plants quickly develop from dormant buds. Even a 1cm (¹/₂in) piece of root left behind is able to regrow.

Rhizomes

Rhizomes are underground stems which can form roots at the 'joints' (nodes) along the stems. If you leave just a small piece of rhizome behind when clearing weeds, dormant buds spring into life at these joints and a new plant quickly begins to develop. Ground elder (p.64) and Japanese knotweed (p.68) are good examples.

Stolons

Look at any bramble (p.54) thicket and you'll notice that the stems arch outwards and downwards, away from the centre of the plant. Look closely and you'll see that the tips of the arching shoots have rooted in the ground – these are called stolons.

These tough rhizomes of ground elder spread just below soil level

A creeping buttercup sending runners in all directions

Runners

Runners are stems on the move, which creep out across the surface of the soil in all directions. Where the stem touches the soil at a node, it quickly sends down roots and a new plant develops. This plant soon begins to send out its own runners, and a sizeable patch soon develops. Creeping buttercup (p.58) spreads in this way and can cover an area of several square metres (square yards) in a single growing season.

Bulbs and bulbils

Anyone who enjoys bluebells (*Hyacinthoides* spp.) in their garden also knows just what a pest they can become. Not only are they prolific seeders, they also increase rapidly underground, soon forming large clumps of tightly packed bulbs. Lesser celandine (*Ranunculus ficaria*), while a spectacle in spring, when its carpets of yellow flowers light up the ground, can wreak havoc in a border, where it quickly spreads and forms colonies of bulbils (miniature corms).

Other survival tactics

Just a fragment of these dandelion taproots can become a whole new plant

- Dandelion (p.60) and curled dock (p.59) send their thick taproots deep into the soil, which helps them survive periods of drought when other, more shallow-rooted weeds are turning brown around them. Although these weeds don't spread vegetatively, if the roots are disturbed and chopped up, each piece is capable of growing into a new plant. Dandelion (p.60) also produces vast numbers of airborne seeds, which is its main way of spreading.

- Lawn weeds such as daisy (p.60) and hoary plantain (p.66) have a flat, spreading growth habit that keeps them just below the blades of your lawn mower. You might succeed in mowing off the flowers, but the growing points remain intact.

- Ragwort (p.74) is poisonous to grazing animals, as is black nightshade (p.52), so they tend to be left well alone.

- The seeds of chickweed (p.56) and groundsel (p.65) can withstand low temperatures and will still germinate after the soil has been frozen solid. In general, the deeper a weed seed lies in the soil, the better its protection from frosts.

- Great bindweed (p.63) and cleavers (p.56) use other plants as supports, weakening and smothering them. They grow very quickly, reaching to where there is plenty of sunlight. Even the humble chickweed (p.56), which keeps on growing through the winter, can swamp crops like spring cabbages.

- Trampling pineapple weed (p.73) and knotgrass (p.69) won't faze them – they are tough weeds well-used to being walked on!

3.

LIVING WITH WEEDS

An earth-friendly approach to weeds is about far more than simply eradicating them from your garden. Of course there will be parts of your garden where you might not want a single weed to grow, but there will always be those unused areas, perhaps where garden plants struggle to grow, that can be left for weeds. If you look again at your garden and think of it as a self-contained miniature 'ecosystem', then living with some weeds makes perfect sense.

The extent to which you are prepared to share your patch with weeds will depend on both you and your garden. You might feel able to give up that hard-to-get-at corner behind the compost bin for a patch of stinging nettle (p.78), or be more ambitious and deliberately include 'wild' patches or strips – aptly named 'bug banks' or 'beetle banks' – in among your more carefully tended beds and borders. Such intentionally wild areas are a magnet for all kinds of wildlife, from beneficial insects such as hoverflies to slug-eating frogs and toads. Boosting populations of beneficial creatures in the garden is just one benefit of harnessing the positive effects which weeds can have – there are many others.

Why weeds can be good for your garden

There are plenty of reasons for preventing and controlling weeds in your garden (see 'Preventing, clearing and controlling weeds', p.81), but also some equally compelling reasons to garden alongside, or even with, weeds:

• Many wild plants (as well as garden plants that can become weeds) are simply beautiful when in flower. They make us feel good!

• Flowering weeds such as creeping thistle (p.59) are an important food source for bees, butterflies, hoverflies and many other beneficial insects. Bees pollinate crops such as runner beans and fruit trees, leading to plentiful harvests. The caterpillars of several butterflies feed on stinging nettle (p.78). Wild areas provide shelter for overwintering insects, amphibians, reptiles and small mammals such as hedgehogs, as well as other

Self-seeded wheat plants often appear unexpectedly if you use a straw mulch, and can be left for the birds

creatures that play an important role in keeping garden pests and diseases in check.

- In spring, germinating weeds are a good indication that the soil is warming up and that it is a suitable time to start sowing seeds outdoors.
- Deep-rooted weeds such as dandelion (p.60) and curled dock (p.59) go deep into the soil, breaking up hard, compacted ground. They also draw valuable plant nutrients to the soil surface, where they can be used by other, more shallow-rooted plants. Composting wilted deep-rooted weeds recycles these valuable nutrients.
- You can eat many common weeds, either raw in salads, like chickweed (p.56) and hairy bittercress (p.65), or in soups, or use them for making beer or wine. See 'Eat your weeds', p.47.
- Weeds make excellent compost – there is no reason why any weeds should go in the rubbish bin. When you pull up a handful of weeds, you grab a bunch of nutrients that can easily be recycled back to your garden plants. Find out how to compost weeds on p.109.

Sun spurge has a warming effect on the soil, encouraging growth in crops like asparagus

- Some weeds, such as sun spurge (p.78), help keep the soil and any nearby plants warm, so have a protective role. Other 'companion' weeds are said to enhance the growth of neighbouring plants, either through secretions from their roots or through the release of chemicals from their leaves and flowers. Others – couch grass (p.38) is a good example – can actually suppress the growth of other plants by excreting chemicals from their roots.
- You can feed your garden with weeds, by using them for making compost or, in the case of stinging nettle (p.78), a rich liquid feed – see p.43.

- Uprooted weeds make an excellent temporary mulch. Covering the ground with a dense layer of wilted weeds stops light reaching the soil surface, prevents other weeds from germinating and helps to stop the soil drying out. Once its job is done, the mulch can be added to the compost bin.
- Self-seeding garden plants which often become weeds, such as pot marigold (p.73) or borage (p.53), need very little work. All you have to do is remove (or transplant) the plants you don't want and leave the others to their own devices.
- Weeds are still a source of raw material for plant breeders. Unusual or distinctive forms of wild plants have been the basis for many of our garden plants.

These self-seeded orange pot marigolds are useful insect attractants, but the tall green fat hen (p.61), willow herb (*Epilobium* spp.) and pale wall barley (*Hordeum murinum*) need removing to stop them seeding

- Allowing weeds to live and reproduce in your garden helps to support not only your garden's ecosystem but the ecosystem of your local area. Remember that weeds have an important role in 'healing' disturbed ground and that their job is to cover bare soil.

Stinging nettle – a weed for all reasons

Every garden, whatever its size, needs a patch of stinging nettles (p.78). Apart from their sting, I find it hard to see any drawbacks to these amazing plants but then, I am a convert to earth-friendly weed control. I also know how easy it is to keep stinging nettles under control. A large spreading clump might look forbidding, but the tough yellow roots don't go that deep into the soil. They are quite easy to fork out and you can always don gloves and cut the tops down first to avoid getting stung. In fact, these plants are incredibly easy to manage and are a sign of fertile soil. Stinging nettles also release (for me at least) a wonderful scent.

Nettles really are multipurpose weeds:

- They make excellent compost material, helping to boost biological activity in a compost heap or bin.
- The young shoot tips can be used to make a tasty, nutritious soup, beer or wine.
- Peacock, small tortoiseshell and red admiral caterpillars feed on the leaves.

Wear gloves to gather the nutritious shoot tips of nettles

Caterpillars of the small tortoiseshell butterfly soon strip the stinging nettle of its leaves

- Leafy shoots can be made into organic liquid plant food – see p.43.
- Clumps of nettles are a favourite haunt of frogs, toads and other wildlife.
- Greenfly (aphids) feeding on the young shoot tips in spring are an important food source for ladybirds coming out of hibernation.
- Nettles have been used for their fibres in the past, and also have medicinal uses.

My stinging nettle patch is neatly contained by the brick base of my shed and grows up between my water butts – an area that would otherwise be unused. Any unused patch of ground or strip of soil can soon be turned into a 'nettle bank', or you can sink bottomless pots or tubs, at least 45cm (18in) wide and 30cm (1ft) deep, into beds and borders and grow your nettles in these. In wide flower borders, clumps of nettles can easily be secluded away at the back, but your garden will still reap the benefits. Any shoots which creep over the sides of the pots are easily removed, so your nettles will stay conveniently contained, just where you want them.

If you have a large patch that you want to reduce in size, cutting the tops back to the ground whenever they reach 45-60cm (18-24in) tall will soon weaken the plants, which will then be easy enough to fork out in the autumn. The tops can be composted or turned into liquid plant food. You can also mulch them out – see p.92.

Feed your garden with weeds

If you have stinging nettles (p.78) in your garden, or can gather them from nearby waste ground, you have all you need to make a nutrient-rich, organic liquid plant food. Nettles collected in spring are particularly high in nitrogen, phosphate and potash. Half-fill a 10-litre (two-gallon) bucket with water, fill it with fresh, leafy nettle tops, top up with water so they are totally immersed, then cover with a lid and wait two weeks. You'll be left with a dark, powerful-smelling liquid feed that should be diluted with 10 parts water before being used as a general garden feed. You can also make this feed in a tub or water butt – use 10 litres (2 gallons) of water to 1kg (2¼lb) of nettle tops, which can be suspended in a mesh bag or old stockings. The decayed nettles can later be added to the compost bin – nothing is wasted.

Grow your own 'bug bank'

Many successful organic farmers and growers, who don't use any synthetic chemical pesticides or weedkillers on their crops, harness nature by including so-called 'bug banks' or 'beetle banks' in their fields. These wild strips are sown with a wide range of wild and cultivated plants. Their purpose is to attract beneficial creatures of all types and to provide a habitat for them. These range from greenfly-eating hoverflies and tiny parasitic wasps that lay their eggs in the caterpillars of large cabbage white and other crop-eating butterflies, to shiny black ground beetles and frogs, both of which forage at night, feeding on slugs.

This 'nettle bank' attracts aphids in early spring, which provide food for ladybirds, while in summer various butterfly caterpillars devour the leaves

The bug bank concept can easily be transferred to your garden, and it can be as simple or as sophisticated as you want. The simplest approach is to let a patch or strip of ground go wild and allow the naturally occurring wild plants to flourish (of course they won't strictly be weeds in this case, as they are growing where you actually want them). The only drawback to a 'see what comes up' approach is that you may discover that there are spreading perennial weeds present, such as great bindweed (p.63), which could invade other parts of your garden. In this case it might be better to actually include a bug bank (or banks) in the overall plan for your garden, which would allow you to deliberately mix together both weeds and garden plants – see 'Useful plants for bug banks', p.46.

The nature of your bug bank will depend on the size, shape and location of your garden. If you live in a rural area, you might discover that surrounding areas of wildflowers act as a ready-made bug bank and that your garden is already filled with wildlife for very little effort. However, in a town or city, you could find yourself in a biological 'desert', hemmed in by neat, weed-free gardens with the frequent whiff of chemical sprays. Here a bug bank will be vital to build a thriving garden ecosystem and allow you to grow flowers, fruit and vegetables in an earth-friendly way. You can boost your garden's biodiversity further by including a pond in your bug bank and providing nesting and breeding sites for beneficial insects and birds.

One of the simplest yet most effective bug banks I know is my own 'nettle bank' around the base of my garden shed – see 'Stinging nettle – a weed for all reasons', p.41.

Some useful plants for bug banks

In general, the wider the range of plants in a bug bank, the better. Where space allows you can include shrubs and even trees. The berries of shrubs such as firethorn (*Pyracantha*) are especially valuable as an autumn and winter food source for birds.

Native/wild plants (weeds):

Bird's-foot trefoil (p.51)
Borage (p.53)
California poppy (p.54)
Canadian golden-rod (p.55)
Curled dock (p.59)
Dandelion (p.60)
Evening primrose (p.61)
Hoary plantain (p.66)
Hogweed (p.67)
Hollyhock (p.67)
Honesty (p.68)
Lady's mantle (p.69)

Lesser hawkbit (p.70)
Love-in-a-mist (p.71)
Nipplewort (p.71)
Opium poppy (p.72)
Pot marigold (p.73)
Redshank (p.74)
Smooth sow thistle (p.77)
Stinging nettle (p.78)
Teasel (p.79)
White clover (p.79)
Yarrow (p.80)

Hogweed's flat 'landing pads' attract important pollinating insects, such as this drone fly (*Eristalis* sp.)

Garden plants:

Angelica (*Angelica archangelica*) P

Annual convolvulus (*Convolvulus tricolor*) A

Asters, including Michaelmas daisy (*Aster* spp.) P

Buckwheat (*Fagopyrum esculentum*) A*

Carrot B

Dill (*Anethum graveolens*) A

Fennel (*Foeniculum vulgare*) P

Ice plant (*Sedum* spp.) P

Lavender (*Lavandula* spp.) P

Lovage (*Levisticum officinale*) P

Mint (*Mentha* spp.) P

Parsnip B

Phacelia (*Phacelia tanacetifolia*) A*

Sunflower (*Helianthus annuus*); avoid pollen-free varieties A

Thyme (*Thymus* spp.) P

Hollyhock will readily self-seed in a bug bank, producing flowers rich in pollen and nectar

A   **Annual**

B   **Biennial – leave rootstock to overwinter, so that plants then produce flowers the following year**

P   **Perennial**

*   **Also grown as a green manure (see p.90)**

Eat your weeds

Many common garden weeds are edible, some are tasty and several are high in health-promoting minerals and vitamins. Some weeds, however, are poisonous; if you are ever in any doubt about the identification of a weed you are thinking of eating, don't take the risk. Eating weeds might not be the most effective method of controlling them, but in the middle of winter, when you're desperate for some fresh greens for a salad, nutritious chickweed (p.56) is ready and waiting to come to the rescue – and it's free.

Edible garden weeds

Use young leaves/shoots raw or cooked:

Chickweed (p.56)

Cleavers (p.56)

Dandelion (p.60) (rich in vitamins A and C)

Evening primrose (p.61) (roots)

Fat hen (p.61) (high in vitamin B)

Hairy bittercress (p.65)

Hoary plantain (p.66)

Hogweed (p.67)

Japanese knotweed (p.68)

Land cress (p.70)

Lesser hawkbit (p.70)

Nipplewort (p.71)

Rosebay willow herb (p.75)

Sheep's sorrel (p.76)

Shepherd's purse (p.77)

Smooth sow thistle (p.77)

Stinging nettle (p.78)

Yarrow (p.80)

Edible flowers/petals:

Borage (p.53)

Evening primrose (p.61)

Hollyhock (p.67)

Pot marigold (p.73)

Edible seeds/fruits:

Bramble (p.54)

Opium poppy (p.72)

Redshank (p.74)

Wine and beer making:

Bramble (p.54) (fruits)

Coltsfoot (p.57) (flowers)

Daisy (p.60) (flowers)

Dandelion (p.60) (flowers)

Stinging nettle (p.78) (leaves)

For books containing more detail on using edible weeds, including recipes, see p.129.

4.

KNOW YOUR WEEDS

Being able to recognise and identify weeds is vital to successful earth-friendly prevention and control. This section looks in detail at 60 common garden weeds, which were all photographed during summer in the English Midlands. The majority are wild plants, both native and introduced to the UK, but I have also included a number of garden plants, such as borage (p.53). This might seem surprising, but borage, along with several other commonly grown garden plants found on the following pages, is entirely capable of becoming a serious weed problem if left unchecked.

This is not an exhaustive list of weeds, but a cross-section found growing in my own garden and allotment (or on nearby plots) and chosen to illustrate the many ways in which weeds grow, spread and survive. Some of these 60 weeds could probably be found in almost any garden in the UK. Hairy bittercress (p.65) has been spread far and wide, largely in the compost used to grow plants sold through nurseries and garden centres. Others, like chickweed (p.56), are also fairly ubiquitous. Some, such as sheep's sorrel (p.76), are found only in areas where the soil is acid.

My choice of weeds has also been influenced by what I have learnt over many years about the ways in which they grow and spread, as well as how they have responded to my attempts to control them. There have been successes and also catastrophic failures and I am still learning. Every garden has its own unique set of challenges.

As you get to know your weeds, understand how they 'tick' and decide how prepared you are to garden alongside them, your skills at accommodating and tackling them will grow.

How the entries are arranged

Throughout this book I have used the 'common' name for each weed with which I am most familiar. Many have several common names. For example, what I know as 'couch grass' (p.58) is also known as 'twitch' or 'squitch'. However, it only has one botanical name – *Elymus repens* – by which it is known throughout the world.

In the pages that follow, the entries are arranged alphabetically by their common names, but the botanical names of all 60 weeds are given as well, so that you can track them down in other sources of information. Examples of other common names (where they exist) are followed by the typical life cycle of the weed (see p.25) and then by an at-a-glance guide to how easy, difficult or urgent dealing with each weed is:

Green	Control easy
Amber	Control moderately easy
Red	Take immediate action to control/prevent spread

For example, say you identify field bindweed (p.62) growing in your garden. This is marked RED because it is a serious perennial weed that can quickly spread by underground roots and needs immediate attention.

Information is also provided on the characteristics of each weed: when/where it is a problem, its size, how it spreads, and any benefits to wildlife and/or to us. Effective control methods are summarised for each weed. Details on preventing, clearing and controlling weeds organically can be found in chapter 5 (p.81).

Annual meadow grass   *Poa annua*

Annual/ephemeral

Growing 5–30cm (2–12in) tall, this little grass can flower and set seed almost year-round. It grows practically everywhere, in paths, beds, borders, kitchen gardens and lawns, where it causes pale patches that suddenly die out, leaving the way open for other lawn weeds to invade. I find it a particular nuisance on my allotment, where it withstands trampling on the paths and is difficult to hoe out, especially if the soil is hard and dry.

Solutions: Hoe seedlings; pull up/fork out large plants; flame gun; mulch.

These flowering plants are surrounded by young seedlings

Bird's-foot trefoil   *Lotus corniculatus*

Other names: eggs and bacon, granny's toenails, hen and chickens

Perennial

This is found in patches in short, rough grass and in lawns, especially around the unmown edges, where it grows 10–30cm (4–12in) tall. The pea-like flowers appear all summer – you may not spot this weed until it actually begins to flower. It is not an especially damaging or troublesome weed unless you want a perfect lawn. The flowers are much visited by bumblebees and its roots add nitrogen to the soil.

Solutions: Encourage healthy grass; mow off shoots.

The long, narrow seed pods, around 2.5cm (1in) long, resemble a bird's 'foot'

Black medick
Medicago lupulina

Annual

This weed can be a pest in lawns and resembles white clover (p.79), although it has smaller heads of yellow flowers from mid-spring to autumn followed by clusters of green, then black, curved seed pods. Shoots can spread 30–60cm (1–2ft) in all directions, smothering out lawn grasses. Being an annual, when black medick dies it leaves bare patches in lawns where other more serious weeds can get a foothold. Odd plants are easy to grub out, but reseed any bare patches.

Solutions: Grub out; encourage grass; mow off.

Black medick thrives in poor-quality lawns like this, where the grass is weak

Black nightshade
Solanum nigrum

Other names: garden nightshade

Annual

All parts of this weed are poisonous. Seeds germinate in late spring and early summer, after frosts. Fully grown plants, 60cm (2ft) tall, produce star-like white flowers from mid-summer onwards, followed by shiny green, then black, fruits from late summer into autumn. Plants are most often found in cultivated parts of the garden where there is bare soil. Remove them as soon as they are spotted, especially if you have young children. This weed is killed by autumn frosts.

Solutions: Hoe; pull up; mulch.

The poisonous, shiny fruits hang from the stems, which are often tinged purple-black

Borage
Borago officinalis
Annual/biennial

Grown as a herb, this prolific self-seeder has escaped in many gardens and should be treated as a weed, except for any plants which you want to allow to develop and flower throughout the summer. Beware though – a fully grown plant can reach 90cm (3ft) tall and wide and soon swamps its neighbours. The bristly-hairy, cucumber-flavoured leaves can irritate skin. Borage is an exceptional plant for attracting bees and other insects. Overwintering rosettes produce the earliest flowers.

Solutions: Hoe; pull up; mulch.

Use the pretty blue flowers to decorate salads or freeze them in ice cubes, or add flowers or young leaves to drinks

Bracken
Pteridium aquilinum
Perennial

Poisonous, tough and invasive, this is a serious weed that has a redeeming quality: the fronds (leaves), if cut in late spring, are excellent for adding to the compost bin and also make a useful, nutrient-rich mulch material. The tough, spreading underground stems are covered in soft brown 'felt' and go around 45cm (18in) deep. The fronds reach 1.8m (6ft) or more tall and die down in winter. Bracken is more likely to be a problem in rural areas.

Solutions: Dig out; persistent treading/ bruising or cutting fronds; mow out; physical barrier.

Wear gloves when cutting or handling bracken in summer and autumn, as it can easily cut your skin

Bramble
Rubus fruticosus agg.

Other names: blackberry

Perennial

This tough, woody weed, with vicious thorns along its arching shoots, attracts a whole host of beneficial creatures, which feed on its pink-white summer flowers and leaves and find a home among its 1.8m (6ft) tall thicket of shoots. The tip of each shoot produces roots when it touches soil, allowing plants to 'leapfrog' into new areas. New plants also grow quickly from seed, scrambling over the ground, creating lethal 'trip wires'.

Solutions: Dig out; long-term sheet mulch.

Gather the delicious ripe fruits in late summer or early autumn for jam- and pie-making

California poppy
Eschscholzia spp.

Annual

California poppy is grown in gardens for its pretty flowers, but can soon spread through borders, earning it weed status. Self-sown seedlings, with their finely divided, blue-grey leaves, are easy to hoe, and large plants pull up without any trouble. It thrives in loose gravel on drives and paths, where using a flame gun is an effective control. Do try to keep as many California poppies as you can – their bright summer flowers attract large numbers of hoverflies to the garden, which prey on pests such as greenfly (aphids).

Solutions: Hoe; pull up; flame gun; mulch.

These are extremely desirable 'weeds' for an earth-friendly garden

Canadian fleabane   *Conyza canadensis*

Other names: horseweed

Annual

Don't let this weed flower – a single plant can release up to 250,000 airborne seeds when flowering begins in mid-summer. It grows on rough, waste ground and in paths and patios, where it will flower and set seed even in very dry conditions. It's worth controlling any plants found outside your garden, such as in or along pavements or even in walls, as its seeds can soon blow into your garden on the slightest breeze. It can irritate skin, so wear gloves.

Solutions: Hoe; pull up; flame gun on paths.

Plants grow 30–60cm (1–2ft) tall and are covered in small, yellow-green flowers

Canadian golden-rod *Solidago canadensis*

Other names: golden-rod

Perennial

When you see just how many bees and other useful insects this plant attracts from late summer onwards, whether to pull it up can be a dilemma! This is an example of a garden plant that can run riot in your garden if not kept in check. Its underground roots can quickly spread, forming a large clump that elbows other plants out. The roots form a tough, impenetrable mass that requires effort to remove – try chopping the roots into chunks first.

Solutions: Dig out; long-term sheet mulch.

Massed heads of small flowers are carried on stems up to 1.5m (5ft) tall

Chickweed *Stellaria media*

Other names: chickwittle, cluckenweed, mischievous Jack

Annual/ephemeral

Dense green clumps of chickweed, up to 30cm (1ft) tall, indicate rich, fertile soil, but it will grow virtually anywhere in the garden, including the cracks in paving. The sprawling stems root as they touch the soil, so large clumps can quickly form, although this is an easy weed to simply pull up in great handfuls. This prolific seeder can produce up to 15,000 seeds per plant. Fresh leafy shoots can be added to salads and are rich in vitamins and minerals.

Solutions: Hoe; pull up; mulch.

The tiny white flowers can appear virtually year-round

Cleavers *Galium aparine*

Other names: goosegrass, stick-a-back, sticky Willie

Annual

Downward-pointing barbed hooks on the leaves and stems allow this fast-growing weed to clamber over other plants, covering them in a dense thicket of shoots up to 1.5m (5ft) long. Small white flowers appear from mid-spring. Kids love to pull off handfuls of these 'sticky' shoots, which cling to clothing, as do the ripe seeds, which are covered in barbed hairs (see p.31). Cleavers is a sign of fertile soil and is easy to control.

Solutions: Hoe; pull up; mulch.

Cleavers in autumn on a holly hedge, showing the faded shoots and the round, sticky seeds

Coltsfoot *Tussilago farfara*

Other names: clayweed, coughwort, foal's foot

Perennial

Pale yellow, daisy-like flowers appear in early to mid-spring, before the leaves start growing, on bare stems 15cm (6in) tall. Dig around these clumps and you'll find thick, white rhizomes, which creep in all directions and go deep into the soil. Persistence will pay off, but if coltsfoot is constantly invading from a neighbouring garden, a physical barrier (see p.86) may be the only option. Don't let the flowers – which can be made into wine – set their airborne seeds.

Solutions: Dig out; long-term sheet mulch; mow out; physical barrier.

The summer leaves are heart-shaped, around 15cm (6in) across, and have a white felting underneath

Common field speedwell *Veronica persica*

Other names: bird's eye, Buxbaum's speedwell

Annual

Creeping over the ground, this is the commonest speedwell found as a garden weed and I find it one of the toughest of all annuals to remove. Its stems run over the soil, rooting as they go and quickly forming a dense wiry mat. I trace the stems back to their origin, loosen the soil and lift out the whole weed. Be vigilant as just a small fragment of stem can root and grow. Plants can produce thousands of fast-germinating seeds and flower from early spring onwards.

Solutions: Hoe; pull up; mulch.

Each sky-blue flower is 1cm (½in) across with a white lower petal

Couch grass *Elymus repens*

Other names: squitch, twitch

Perennial

This is an aggressive weed that can become a serious nuisance because of its spreading, brittle rhizomes, which find their way into nooks and crannies in paths and which weave themselves happily among border plants. The tough rhizomes can form a dense mat just below the surface, although I find them relatively easy to fork out as they don't go too deep. Plants can regrow from a tiny fragment; wait until you see new leaves, then loosen the soil underneath and carefully lift the young plant out with as much root as possible.

Solutions: Fork out; long-term sheet mulch; physical barrier.

The sharp-pointed, wiry rhizomes can puncture potatoes and grow through them

Creeping buttercup *Ranunculus repens*

Perennial

Bright yellow flowers appear all summer on plants up to 60cm (2ft) tall, which are usually found on moist soils. Plants soon swamp neighbours if left unchecked, but are quite easy to remove if you loosen the soil beneath them first with a fork – they have masses of tough, white roots anchoring them to the ground. Their main means of spread is by fast-growing runners that travel over the surface of the ground. Plants can also invade and spread through damp, patchy lawns. They are poisonous if eaten.

Solutions: Hoe seedlings; fork out large plants; long-term sheet mulch.

Fast-growing runners spread out in all directions, rooting at each joint (node) on the stem

Creeping thistle   *Cirsium arvense*

Perennial

Don't delay in starting to control this serious weed. Fleshy white taproots go deep into the ground, but also send out creeping roots horizontally. Where these touch the surface, narrow, spiny leaves form on a new shoot, which grows 60–150cm (2–5ft) tall and flowers in summer. Later, the heads release masses of soft, fluffy down (see p.28), containing the tiny airborne seeds. To remove as much root as possible, loosen the soil then ease the whole plant out – even a tiny root fragment will regrow. Persistence will pay off.

Solutions: Fork/dig out; physical barrier; long-term sheet mulch.

Bees and butterflies are drawn to the sweet-scented flowers

Curled dock   *Rumex crispus*

Other names: crisped dock

Perennial

All docks are problematic weeds, all with thick taproots going deep into the ground. The narrow leaves of curled dock have distinctive wavy edges and plants can reach 90cm (3ft) tall. A single large plant is able to produce 30,000 seeds in one season, half of which are still able to germinate after 50 years, making this 'pioneer' weed one of the first to begin colonising bare soil. Dock seedlings hoe off easily until their roots become 1cm (½in) or more thick.

Solutions: Hoe seedlings; fork/dig out taproots; long-term sheet mulch.

In summer, spikes of reddish seeds follow the greenish flowers

Daisy *Bellis perennis*

Other names: bairnwort, day's eye

Perennial

Few sights match a ground-hugging carpet of daisy flowers in spring and summer, but in your lawn it may not be so welcome! Tackling daisies is challenging; try letting the grass grow longer, to help smother the daisies, or grub out individuals. For larger patches, cut out sections of affected turf and lay fresh turf or reseed, but make sure you remove every trace as this weed spreads using ground-hugging runners, as well as by seed.

Solutions: Hoe; fork out; grub out (lawns).

Each flower is up to 2.5cm (1in) across and sits above spoon-shaped leaves

Dandelion *Taraxacum officinale*

Other names: blow balls, pee-a-bed, wet-a-bed

Perennial

Dandelion's deep taproot must be dug or forked out and older plants, with very deep roots, may need several attempts. However, dandelion doesn't spread sideways, so I let a few plants produce their bright yellow flowers, on stalks up to 30cm (1ft) tall, as a useful food source for insects in early spring – but I nip the green seed-heads off before they turn into 'clocks' (see p.29) and release their airborne seeds. Dandelion quickly colonises bare soil. Use the flowers for wine, the young leaves (rich in vitamins A and C) for salads.

Solutions: Hoe seedlings; fork/dig out; long-term sheet mulch; mulch.

Add the wilted, nutrient-rich taproots and flat rosettes to your compost bin or weed bags

Evening primrose   *Oenothera biennis*

Biennial

These are beautiful garden plants, but they self-seed like mad and soon become tiresome invaders, with deep, tough taproots that can take some removing. They readily escape from gardens, will grow virtually anywhere and are often found on waste ground and roadsides. In summer young plants form flat rosettes of narrow leaves, which will flower the following year, so simply remove any young plants growing where you don't want them. The scented, 8cm (3in) wide flowers are much visited by insects, especially moths.

Solutions: Hoe; pull up; fork out; mulch.

New flowers open each evening then gradually fade the following day

Fat hen   *Chenopodium album*

Other names: bacon weed, drought weed, wild spinach

Annual

This 'pioneer' weed is among the first to grow on disturbed ground, in the gardens of newly built houses and near manure heaps. It thrives in dry soils. Plants are covered in a mealy white coating, which glistens in the sun. Flowering is from early summer until autumn and, if not pulled up, a large plant can shed up to 20,000 seeds into the soil. Fat hen will reach 90–180cm (3–6ft) – larger plants are a sign of fertile soil.

Solutions: Hoe; pull up; mulch.

Cook the nutritious leafy tops of young plants like this in the same way as spinach

Field bindweed
Convolvulus arvensis

Other names: devil's gut, lesser bindweed

Perennial

With roots penetrating up to 10m (30ft) deep into the soil, this is a serious weed in all situations, and a tiny root fragment can regrow. You might not know you have field bindweed until its pinkish shoots appear in spring. The entwining shoots, with arrow-shaped leaves, can grow to 1.8m (6ft) and will swamp any other plant. Its presence indicates deep, fertile soil.

Solutions: Persistent hoeing (to weaken); dig out all traces of roots; long-term sheet mulch; mow out.

Although the flowers are attractive to insects, avoid letting plants flower as a single plant can produce more than 500 seeds

Field horsetail
Equisetum arvense

Other names: cat's tail, pipeweed

Perennial

With black, wiry rhizomes reaching more than 2m (6ft) deep, this pernicious weed is extremely hard, and on occasion virtually impossible, to eradicate from the garden, especially if plants are constantly invading from elsewhere. In early to mid-spring, brown cones appear on bare stems, followed in summer by ferny green 25–30cm (10–12in) tall shoots that feel rough to the touch. Its presence indicates compacted ground and, in some cases, poor drainage. Persistent hoeing will weaken horsetail, but growing taller plants to smother it is also effective.

Solutions: Hoe; fork/dig out; long-term sheet mulch.

Here field horsetail is pushing up, from deep below ground, in a vegetable garden

Giant hogweed *Heracleum mantegazzianum*

Other names: cartwheel plant, giant cow parsnip

Biennial

This potentially dangerous weed is spectacular to look at but toxic to touch, and it can be an offence to grow or plant it in some areas. The problem lies in chemicals in the sap, which make skin hypersensitive to sunlight, causing long-lived, painful blisters and scarring. Avoid letting children play near giant hogweed and remove young plants as soon as possible, digging out all traces of the roots. Plants flower in mid- to late summer and can reach 5m (16ft) tall with flower-heads 50cm (20in) across.

Solutions: Fork/dig out; mulch.

Never touch the huge, divided leaves, or the speckled stems, which can blister the skin

Great bindweed *Calystegia silvatica*

Other names: hellweed, lady-jump-out-of-bed, large bindweed, woodbine

Perennial

Clambering up to 3m (10ft) tall, entwining and smothering other plants and with roots going deep into the soil, this is a serious weed. Its shoots will run over bare ground until they find a support and it will also smother hedges, shrubs and trees. Plants can regenerate from tiny fragments of white root. Look out for pink-tinged new shoots in spring, attached to thick white roots. Avoid getting the irritant sap on your skin.

Solutions: Dig out all traces of roots; long-term sheet mulch; physical barrier.

Flowers up to 8cm (3in) across appear all summer among heart-shaped leaves

Great willow herb — *Epilobium hirsutum*

Other names: codlins and cream

Perennial

Damp soil near ponds is a favourite haunt of this tough weed, which spreads using its thick, white rhizomes and by releasing thousands of airborne seeds. It can also be found invading beds and borders. Plants reach 1.5m (5ft) when in flower and soon form dense clumps if left unchecked. This weed is often a problem in an overgrown garden, but it will also invade your plot by travelling under boundary fences from waste ground, so try using a physical barrier.

Solutions: Hoe; fork/dig out; long-term sheet mulch

Flowers appear from early summer and are followed by tiny seeds attached to silky threads

Ground elder — *Aegopodium podagraria*

Other names: bishop's weed, goutweed, jack-jump-about

Perennial

Often found entrenched beneath shady hedge bottoms, where its spreading rhizomes are difficult to eradicate, this weed can cause serious problems. However, the pale underground rhizomes don't go deep and are quite easy to remove. On a large area, sheet mulching is more practical, or you could try persistent mowing out. In summer, plants up to 90cm (3ft) tall produce heads of white flowers, followed by seeds that scatter in all directions. You can cook the young leaves like spinach.

Solutions: Fork/dig out; mow out; long-term sheet mulch; physical barrier.

The shiny green summer foliage is aromatic if crushed

Groundsel
Senecio vulgaris

Other names: birdseed, switchen

Annual/ephemeral

Don't let this prolific weed flower and release its airborne seeds – a single plant can produce over 1,000 seeds and can flower in any month of the year! Easy to pull up, plants grow 8–45cm (3–18in) tall, larger plants indicating rich, fertile soil – a good sign in a newly inherited garden or allotment. The small, petalless flowers resemble yellow brushes. This weed is sometimes attacked by orange-coloured rust disease, but pull it up whenever you see it, or hoe off the seedlings. Birds feed on the seeds.

Solutions: Hoe; pull up; mulch.

Groundsel soon colonises bare soil and can flower and set seed in just five weeks

Hairy bittercress
Cardamine hirsuta

Annual/ephemeral

Plant producers and gardeners are the main means by which this troublesome little weed spreads. Just a single dormant seed or plant in the top of a pot, if allowed to flower and set seeds, can infest an entire garden. Once established, the explosive pods fling the seeds up to 90cm (3ft) in all directions. The seeds are also sticky when wet and cling to boots. It will grow almost anywhere. Use the tasty leaves raw in salads.

Solutions: Hoe; pull up; scrape the top 2.5cm (1in) of compost from new plants; mulch.

Plants grow around 15cm (6in) tall and flower from late spring to early winter

Himalayan balsam *Impatiens glandulifera*

Other names: bee bums, Indian balsam, policeman's helmet

Annual

Clumps of this highly invasive weed fill the air with the scent of ripe plums in late summer. It thrives in damp soil, especially near ponds, rivers and streams. Although it is a summer magnet for bumblebees and other insects, I have seen plants reach over 2.5m (8ft) tall and swamp all other plants around them. Fortunately, young plants are easy to hoe or pull up, which should be done long before any flowers appear. For more on this weed see p.30.

Solutions: Hoe; pull up; mulch.

These large green seed pods are ready to explode, throwing the seeds up to 5m (16ft)

Hoary plantain *Plantago media*

Other names: lamb's tongue

Perennial

You won't see the pretty pink flowers of this common lawn weed unless you don't mow for several weeks. The plantains are serious weeds in lawns, with tough roots and wide, spreading leaves that smother the grass. Mowing only removes the flowers and clips the edges of the leaves. To eradicate them from a small lawn, deal with each rosette individually by severing the roots as far down in the soil as possible, then reseed the bare patch left behind.

Solutions: Grub out; encourage grass growth.

Lawn grasses are soon edged out by the flat rosettes of greyish, hairy leaves

Hogweed *Heracleum sphondylium*

Other names: cow parsnip, keck, limberscrimps

Biennial/perennial

Often seen on roadsides, this tough, taprooted weed can be difficult to remove if it gets a foothold in beds or borders. Leafy rosettes of deeply lobed leaves grow first, which then overwinter before producing flowering shoots up to 3m (10ft) tall. Hogweed is ideal for a 'bug bank' because insects flock to the flat 'landing pad' flower-heads, and you can easily cut off the unripe seeds. Don't get the sap on your skin – like giant hogweed, it can cause severe blistering.

Solutions: Hoe; fork/dig out; mulch.

The 20cm (8in) wide umbrella-like flower-heads are a magnet for beneficial hoverflies and appear from late spring

Hollyhock *Alcea rosea*

Biennial

Hollyhocks are so beautiful that it's hard to label them as weeds. But so good are they at self-seeding that sometimes you do need to rein them back. Seeds will germinate almost anywhere, including between the cracks in paving. Remove any plants you don't want by pulling up the leafy rosettes from spring onwards – these produce tall flower spikes up to 2.5m (8ft) tall the following summer – but try to leave some plants to attract beneficial insects, especially bees. Flower colour varies.

Solutions: Hoe; fork out; flame gun; mulch.

Flowers are up to 10cm (4in) across and the petals can be added to salads

Honesty   *Lunaria annua*

Other names: bread-and-cheese, moonpennies

Biennial

Easy to pull up, this is another pretty garden plant that needs to be kept in check to prevent it swamping other plants. Heads of purple (sometimes white) flowers appear from mid-spring and are a useful nectar source for butterflies as they come out of hibernation, so allow a few plants, which grow 60–90cm (2–3ft) tall, to flower. Self-sown seedlings around the base of plants are easy to hoe off, or you can transplant small clumps to other parts of the garden.

Solutions: Hoe; pull up; mulch.

Semi-transparent honesty seed pods in summer – the large flat seeds can be seen inside

Japanese knotweed   *Fallopia japonica*

Perennial

This is such a serious weed that in some areas it can be an offence to grow or spread it in the wild. It has thick, woody rhizomes that spread quickly in all directions. Even a tiny fragment can grow again; it can also spread by seed. In spring the young shoots quickly grow into zig-zagging stems 2.5m (8ft) in height. Eradication is very difficult. Dig out small clumps, cut plants down every two to three weeks over several years to weaken them, or try sheet mulching. For more on why this weed can be friend and foe, see p.23.

Solutions: Dig out; cut down; mow out; long-term sheet mulch.

Heads of creamy-white flowers, which attract hordes of insects, appear in late summer

Knotgrass

Polygonum aviculare

Other names: prostrate knotweed, redlegs, wireweed

Annual

This common, spreading weed, with its wiry green stems and tiny, pink-white summer flowers, grows flat on the ground on bare soil, in borders or, as seen here, in paths, where it is tough enough to withstand constant trampling. Unlike many annual weeds, it sends a taproot 30–60cm (1–2ft) deep into the soil and will soon regrow if you hoe the top of the plant off. Often found on drier, sandy soils, knotgrass spreads by seeds, which can lie dormant for many years.

Solutions: Hoe; fork/dig out; mulch.

Grub out plants in paths, removing as much root as possible

Lady's mantle

Alchemilla mollis

Perennial

This is one of several perennial garden plants that can quickly become weeds. Lady's mantle spreads far and wide by producing large quantities of seeds, and the resulting seedlings soon smother other plants. Seeds will also germinate in cracks in paths. Seeding is drastically reduced by cutting off the summer flower-heads when they start to go over and turn brown – simply grab bunches of stems and trim them off with secateurs or give plants a haircut using shears. Flowering plants reach 50cm (20in) tall.

Solutions: Hoe; dig out; mulch.

If left, these self-sown seedlings (foreground) will soon swamp this narrow border

Land cress
Barbarea verna

Other names: American cress, early yellowrocket, upland cress

Biennial

Grown for its hot and peppery leaves, this winter salad plant will send up shoots 30–40cm (12–16in) tall in spring, topped with yellow flowers, followed by narrow pods packed with seeds. If allowed to self-seed, it produces masses of fast-growing seedlings which soon smother other plants. Each plant grows into a flat, overwintering rosette of dark green, pinnate leaves. To stop it flowering and self-seeding, eat it constantly, then pull up and compost old plants in spring.

Solutions: Hoe; fork/dig out; pull up.

Harvest the leaves in winter, but remove plants before they flower

Lesser hawkbit
Leontodon taraxacoides

Perennial

You may not know you have this weed in your lawn, until it goes for several weeks without being mown. Only then, as with many other lawn weeds, do the plants have the chance to flower properly (regular mowing removes the flower-buds before they can develop). Its creeping mats of usually hairy, lobed leaves smother out lawn grasses and indicate a dry, often sandy soil. Encouraging stronger grass growth and letting the grass grow longer will smother out lesser hawkbit, or you can grub out small patches and reseed.

Solutions: Grub out; encourage grass; replace turf.

The daisy-like flowers are 1–2cm ($1/2$–$3/4$in) across and appear from early summer to early autumn

Love-in-a-mist   *Nigella damascena*

Annual

Growing around 30cm (1ft) tall, love-in-a-mist is widely grown for its pretty blue summer flowers, but it can quickly seed itself as a weed in sunny spots all around your garden. Each fat, hollow seed pod is filled with black seeds that germinate quickly once they reach the soil, producing carpets of pale green seedlings with distinctive narrow leaves. Hoe at this stage to remove any plants you don't want, or simply pull up any larger plants. Young plants that germinate in autumn will usually survive over winter.

Solutions: Hoe; pull up; flame gun; mulch.

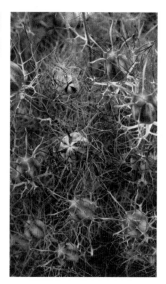

In late summer the inflated, hollow seed pods nestle among the fine, divided leaves

Nipplewort   *Lapsana communis*

Annual/biennial

A common weed, indicating heavy soil, that can grow to 90cm (3ft) tall, nipplewort has small, dandelion-like flowers from late spring onwards, which close up in late afternoon. Each plant can shed 1,000 seeds, so controlling plants while young will reduce future problems. Seeds germinate in autumn and spring; a flat rosette of lyre-shaped leaves forms before flowering begins. I find winter a good time to tackle nipplewort by slicing off the tops of the rosettes with a sharp hoe. The young leaves, although bitter, can be used in salads.

Solutions: Hoe; pull up; mulch.

A flowering plant in late afternoon, its blooms now closed up for the day

Opium poppy   *Papaver somniferum*

Annual

Growing 90–120cm (3–4ft) tall, this colourful poppy has escaped from gardens and is now a widespread weed on waste ground. The commonest flower colour is pink, but other shades sometimes appear, including white. Flowering begins in early summer. Expect plants to appear wherever you cultivate soil – the tiny seeds can lie dormant in the soil for 100 years. Seedlings are easy to spot by their blue-grey leaves. Young plants will often overwinter, flowering the following summer. Avoid getting the poisonous sap on your skin.

Solutions: Hoe; pull up; mulch.

Cut off the seed capsules while still green and unripe, to avoid more seeds being shed

Pearlwort   *Sagina procumbens*

Other names: procumbent pearlwort

Perennial

Easily mistaken for moss, this low-growing weed will colonise the gaps between paving stones or slabs, even in shade, and is troublesome in damp lawns. It also makes densely woven mats on bare, cultivated soil and spreads by creeping shoots as well as by its tiny, dust-like seeds, which are spread by the wind. Tiny white flowers open from late spring. Use a flame gun to tackle it on paths, although you may need to repeat the treatment several times. In lawns, allow grass to grow taller.

Solutions: Hoe; pull up; flame gun; mulch.

This seeding plant is growing on bare soil, forming a dense dark green mat

Pineapple weed *Matricaria discoidea*

Other names: pineapple mayweed, rayless mayweed

Annual

Rubbing the feathery leaves of this widespread weed releases its tell-tale scent of pineapple. It grows almost anywhere, but especially on compacted soil and well-trodden paths, where it resists trampling. Plants flower from late spring until autumn and can be from 5–40cm (2–16in) tall. Over 5,000 seeds can be produced by a single plant, which quickly germinate on the soil surface. I find that a razor-sharp hoe easily skims plants from rock-hard paths.

Solutions: Hoe; pull up; mulch.

This weed is easy to tell by its lack of petals – each flower is a small, greenish-yellow button

Pot marigold *Calendula officinalis*

Annual

Pot marigolds are an essential element in an earth-friendly garden, being one of the best plants for attracting beneficial insects, including bees, hoverflies and butterflies. They are also prolific self-seeders and can become irksome weeds. Fortunately control is very easy, at any time of the year. Bushy plants up to 60cm (2ft) tall begin flowering in late spring and last all summer. Seeds are shed in late summer and autumn; the resulting seedlings then overwinter and flower the following summer. Seeds also germinate in spring as the soil warms up.

Solutions: Hoe; pull up; mulch.

Scatter the edible petals of pot marigold on summer salads

Ragwort
Jacobaea vulgaris

Other names: fellon weed, stagger weed

Biennial

Poisonous to animals, including horses, ragwort usually grows on poor, dry soils and can invade gardens using its airborne seeds. It will grow almost anywhere and can even take hold in a lawn, where in the first year it forms a flat rosette of toothed, ragged leaves. Flowers appear in flat-topped clusters from mid-summer on plants reaching up to 90cm (3ft) tall. The striped caterpillars of the cinnabar moth feed on the leaves. Fork out any rosettes you find, along with the roots.

Solutions: Hoe; fork/dig out; mulch.

Can you spot the orange and black caterpillars?

Redshank
Persicaria maculosa

Other names: persicaria, red spot, willow weed

Annual

To identify this fast-growing weed, look for the dark, arrowhead-shaped spots on the leaves and for pink flowers, which appear non-stop from early summer until autumn. This leafy weed grows anywhere in the garden, often among vegetable crops, but you can also find it at pond edges or where muddy puddles form, where it thrives in the moist conditions. Seeds germinate in spring and early summer, the seedlings being quite easy to spot from an early age.

Solutions: Hoe; pull up; mulch.

Plants usually reach 25–45cm (10–18in) tall and flower at the tips of the shoots

Rosebay willow herb *Chamerion angustifolium*

Other names: bombweed, fireweed

Perennial

On hot, dry days in late summer the air is filled with the fluffy airborne seeds of this weed – one plant can produce 100,000 seeds – but it's the tough, white rhizomes that you need to remove for effective control. Large colonies of rosebay willow herb are found on waste ground (often after a fire) and in churchyards. Flower spikes reach 1.2–1.5m (4–5ft) in mid-summer with long, narrow leaves lower down. If your garden is invaded from rough ground, use a physical barrier buried in the soil.

Solutions: Fork/dig out; physical barrier; long-term sheet mulch.

Below the flowers are the long, narrow seed pods

Scarlet pimpernel *Anagallis arvensis*

Other names: bird's tongue, John-go-to-bed-at-noon, poor man's weather-glass

Annual

Now banished by weedkillers to field margins, this pretty little weed is often found in gardens and allotments, especially at path and border edges. It is easy to identify from its pale scarlet flowers and square stems. The five pointed petals earn it one of its common names, 'bird's tongue'. Plants usually flop out over the soil, reaching 5–10cm (2–4in) in height. They flower from early to mid-summer. Hoeing is effective, although larger plants are often better pulled up.

Solutions: Hoe; pull up; mulch.

Flowers open on dry, fine days but close by late afternoon, or when it is dull or wet

Self-heal
Prunella vulgaris

Perennial

Runners that root where they touch the soil allow this lawn weed to grow into large, dark green patches. Close mowing only encourages it to flower low down, below the reach of the mower blades. This is a difficult weed to eradicate from a lawn, especially if it has spread extensively. Small patches can be grubbed out by hand; consider replacing larger areas. That said, this is a pretty lawn weed that does no real harm and is visited by bees and other insects during the summer.

Solutions: Grub out; replace turf.

In this lawn, self-heal flowers happily below the mower blades from late spring onwards

Sheep's sorrel
Rumex acetosella

Perennial

Indicating poor, acid soil with a low pH, this weed is found in many lawns and is easily identified by its arrow-shaped leaves. Plants have deep taproots making them tough to grub out and they also spread using creeping underground roots. Red-yellow heads of flowers appear on 30cm (1ft) tall stems from late spring onwards – but not in a closely mown lawn. Sheep's sorrel can be difficult to banish from a lawn unless you improve fertility to encourage stronger grass growth, and raise the pH.

Solutions: Grub out; encourage grass.

Add the young, arrow-shaped leaves to salads for an acid, tangy flavour

Shepherd's purse   *Capsella bursa-pastoris*

Other names: pepper and salt, pickpocket

Annual/ephemeral

This is one of our commonest weeds and can be found in flower virtually year-round. In gardens it favours bare, cultivated soil and anywhere that the soil has been disturbed, reaching up to 40cm (16in) tall. Seeds that germinate in autumn form flat, leafy rosettes, which overwinter and then flower the following spring. Young shoots can be added to salads. This weed is a host for white blister, a fungal disease affecting members of the brassica family, such as Brussels sprouts, so keep it out of your vegetable garden.

Solutions: Hoe; pull up; mulch.

Triangular-shaped seed pods earn this weed its common name

Smooth sow thistle   *Sonchus oleraceus*

Other names: hare's lettuce, milk thistle, milkweed

Annual

A deep taproot makes this weed hard to remove, especially on hard ground, so loosen the soil first. Never allow plants to flower – a single plant can release over 5,000 airborne seeds. Yellow flowers appear in clusters from early summer onwards, on branching plants 25–90cm (10–36in) tall. Autumn-germinating seeds produce leafy, overwintering rosettes. The five-sided stems are hollow and release white sap when broken. This weed is a sign of rich, fertile soil and is common on cultivated ground.

Solutions: Hoe; pull up; mulch.

Despite its forbidding appearance, this weed has only soft spines on its leaves

Stinging nettle — *Urtica dioica*

Other names: devil's plaything, Jinny nettle

Perennial

Well-known for their painful sting, these weeds are widespread and extremely useful in an organic garden – discover their many benefits and uses on p.41. New shoots appear in spring from thick, yellow roots that form a dense mat just below the surface. The stems can reach 1.5m (5ft) tall and form dense thickets, often on the sites of old bonfires or a forgotten compost/manure heap, and are useful indicators of fertile ground. The tough roots don't go deep and are fairly easy to fork out.

Solutions: Fork/dig out; physical barrier; long-term sheet mulch.

Tassel-like flowers appear from early summer onwards and are wind-pollinated

Sun spurge — *Euphorbia helioscopia*

Other names: cat's milk, milkwort, wartweed

Annual

Recently cultivated soil is where you can expect to see this easily identified weed; look out for its pale green, hairless leaves and dome-shaped heads of greenish-yellow flowers that appear from mid-spring until autumn. Plants grow to around 30cm (1ft) tall and wide. Its fibrous roots make this weed easy to pull up, but always wear gloves as the sticky white sap can lead to blisters or skin irritation, especially on a sunny day. Try hoeing plants off first, then collecting them up after they've wilted.

Solutions: Hoe; pull up (wear gloves); mulch.

A distinctive whorl of five stems carry the flowers

Teasel
Dipsacus fullonum

Other names: brushes and combs, Venus' basin

Biennial

Only treat teasel as a 'weed' if it interferes with your gardening as it has many benefits. In late summer plants reach 1.2–1.5m (4–5ft) tall and are topped with conical heads that are magnets for bees and butterflies. Insects drink rainwater collected in the leaf bases, while in autumn and winter goldfinches visit the brown heads for their seeds. Loosen the soil around plants you don't want and remove as much root as possible. Try to tolerate a few of these weeds at the back of borders – although they are aggressive self-seeders.

Solutions: Fork/dig out; mulch.

The prickly dome-shaped heads are a mass of smaller flowers

White clover
Trifolium repens

Other names: Dutch clover

Perennial

It is loved by bees, so think twice before removing this pretty weed. In cultivated ground clover will send out runners and soon form a thick mat of growth that is hard to hoe off, so loosen the plant with a fork first and remove it whole. Nodules on the roots are rich in nitrogen, making this an excellent weed for the compost bin. In lawns, plants will still flower even with regular close mowing. Elsewhere, plants can reach 15cm (6in) tall and flower from late spring until autumn.

Solutions: Hoe; fork out large plants; mulch.

Bees are drawn to the scented, nectar-rich flowers

Yarrow
Achillea millefolium

Other names: milfoil

Perennial

Rub the leaves of this weed to release its aroma. Yarrow is mostly a problem in lawns, where it smothers lawn grasses and spreads by creeping stems. On ragged lawn edges (or in a bug bank) flat heads of white flowers appear from early summer on 15–45cm (6–18in) tall stems. It also spreads by seed. Control is difficult in a lawn unless you can grub out localised patches or replace sections of turf. If yarrow invades borders, fork it out.

Solutions: Fork/dig out (borders); grub out; replace turf.

In this closely mown lawn the fine, feathery leaves make a spreading mat

Yellow oxalis
Oxalis corniculata

Other names: creeping lady's sorrel, procumbent yellow sorrel

Annual/perennial

Along lawn edges, in patchy lawns and on bare, cultivated soil is where you are likely to find this creeping weed. Its small flowers, barely 5mm (¼in) across, appear from late spring until autumn, followed by pointed seed pods, which explode, scattering the seeds. Remove larger plants by loosening the soil first and pulling them up. In lawns, grub them out, reseed bare patches and let the grass grow taller to smother this annoying little weed.

Solutions: Hoe; fork out; pull up; mulch.

Plants soon form spreading mats of shamrock-like leaves

5.

PREVENTING, CLEARING AND CONTROLLING WEEDS

The earth-friendly approach to preventing, clearing and controlling weeds isn't simply a matter of letting nature take over your garden – it's about allowing it in a little more and working alongside it so that both you and nature benefit. That said, even organic gardeners need to keep on top of weeds. This chapter looks at how and why weeds can cause problems, and at earth-friendly ways of preventing, clearing and controlling weeds in different situations.

Whether you've just pushed your way through a thicket of weeds in a new garden, or you've recently decided to adopt a safer, more earth-friendly gardening ethos, it's helpful to understand the basic principles that underpin the organic approach to dealing with weeds.

- **Know your weeds**. By identifying a weed, you can look up its life cycle and decide when and how to deal with it.
- **Eliminate by design**. Design your garden – or separate areas within it – to include features that help prevent weeds, such as ground cover (see p.88).
- **Suit yourself**. Use methods of weed prevention, clearance and control to suit the amount of time and energy you have available.
- **Adopt a 'covered earth' policy from the start**. Never leave soil bare; cover it with mulch, or use ground cover plants or a green manure crop. Mulches in particular are the earth-friendly gardener's greatest asset and usually require little effort – see p.92.

These runner beans are growing well above the thicket of weeds on this allotment, but other, lower-growing crops are being swamped

- **Tackle the problem in bite-size chunks**. Be realistic and divide your garden up into several different areas, then use weed prevention and clearance techniques as appropriate. There is nothing more disheartening than failing to get on top of a garden or allotment full of weeds. Weed-beating sheet mulches (see p.96) are invaluable for clearing almost any area of weeds.
- **Be thorough**. Take your time when clearing ground of perennial weeds ahead of any permanent planting.
- **Patience does pay**. It may take a little extra thought, planning and time, but you can prevent and control weeds effectively without weedkillers. Pro-weedkiller enthusiasts often decry the organic approach to dealing with weeds, claiming it takes 'too long' to be effective.

Weeds will invade a greenhouse – it will now take hard work to remove the tough roots of these docks and great bindweed

A few weeks after this picture was taken, the self-seeded borage plants (right) had completely swamped this courgette and cropping had stopped

This border has been overwhelmed by great bindweed. Look closely and you can just see the lights along the edge of the path

Why are weeds a problem?

We've already seen how some weeds can have benefits in the garden and can be an important part of your garden's overall ecosystem. But there comes a time in every garden, young or old, when weeds start to cause problems:

- They compete with garden plants for light, moisture and nutrients, causing weak growth, which is prone to pests and diseases.
- Yields, especially of vegetable and salad crops, can be severely reduced when plants are swamped by weeds. Flowering can be ruined if weeds take a hold among bedding plants or in mixed borders.
- The appearance of your garden plants is soon spoiled by pernicious weeds such as great bindweed (p.63), which clambers up plants, strangling them with its twining shoots. Weeds in a lawn can spoil its appearance – although this does depend on your idea of what a lawn should be like (see 'Weeds in lawns', p.111).
- Ponds and bog and stream gardens can become choked by moisture-loving weeds such as Himalayan balsam (p.66). Weeds with tough underground parts can disturb and puncture pond liners.

Clearing the tough wiry stems and thick white roots of great bindweed makes harvesting potatoes a chore

- Weeds can make harvesting crops and gathering cut flowers difficult – painful, even, if stinging nettles (p.78) are invading your garden.
- Some weeds, such as chickweed (p.56), act as a 'reservoir' for virus diseases, helping them survive from year to year. Even the seeds of chickweed can carry viruses, so when a new plant grows, the virus can be transferred to your garden plants by sap-sucking insects. Clubroot, a serious fungal disease affecting brassicas like cabbage or wallflower, can survive on the roots of shepherd's purse (p.77), then infect susceptible crops planted nearby.
- Hardy overwintering weeds can harbour colonies of insect pests, such as greenhouse whitefly, which then move on to crops in spring.
- Certain weeds are poisonous. The sap of sun spurge (p.78) and giant hogweed (p.63) can cause skin blisters while all parts of black nightshade (p.52) are toxic.

- The powerful underground parts of weeds like Japanese knotweed (p.68) can damage patios, paths, drives and walls – also see p.23.

This list is not meant to be exhaustive. There will always be unexpected problems in your own garden, which has its own unique set of conditions and weeds.

Having identified the problems caused by weeds, we can now turn to the earth-friendly approach to dealing with them, which is divided into three parts. The first looks at how to prevent weeds from becoming a problem, and is essential reading for anyone taking on a brand new house and garden, or if you are planning to redevelop part of your plot. 'Clearing weed-infested ground' looks at techniques you can use to clear a badly overgrown garden or allotment of established weeds and includes details of 'sheet mulching' – an effective way to clear weeds without back-breaking digging. Finally, we look at how to control the everyday weeds, which will appear in any garden from time to time.

Japanese knotweed, which is growing at the top of this wall, has sent its tough rhizomes downwards and is starting to cause structural damage

Preventing weeds

Preventing weeds is the number one priority in any garden or allotment. Put prevention at the top of your list if you take on a brand new house and garden, where plenty of bare soil is a weed invasion waiting to happen. Don't worry too much about designing the garden at this stage, just get it covered up – see 'Mulch magic', p.92. In an established garden there's a good chance that weeds will be under control, or at least restricted to specific areas. Preventing weeds is all about outwitting them before they become a problem.

Security check

In general, plants from garden centres and nurseries will be free of serious perennial weeds, but they could still be carrying fast-spreading annuals such as hairy bittercress (p.65), or their dormant seeds, in the compost. If weeds – or flat green liverworts – are growing in the compost in a pot, scrape off the top 2.5cm (1in) of compost and either bury it in the garden or put it in the dustbin.

Serious perennial weeds such as great bindweed (p.63) can spread unseen, hidden among the roots of perennial garden plants. If you're offered plants from another garden, check them over carefully before planting. If you spot any roots that are obviously not part of the plant you want, wash the soil away and remove any suspicious root fragments. As an extra precaution, grow the plant on in a pot for a few months – any perennial weeds will grow too and can be removed.

The right start

Raising young plants in pots or module trays gets them off to a flying start and helps them compete with any weeds far better after they are planted out. Use organic, peat-free compost to raise plants and to keep them well fed. Planting into weed-free, mulched ground will reduce any problems dramatically.

Shut them out

Using physical barriers to deter weeds is very effective in many gardens. The simplest barriers are hedges and fences, which help deflect wind and any airborne weed seeds. If neighbouring gardens have spreading perennial weeds or they are invading from wild areas outside your garden, a vertical barrier buried

45–60cm (18–24in) deep can be highly effective against spreading roots. First dig a trench along your boundary or fence bottom, then lay your barrier in it and replace the soil, so it sits just proud of the surface. I find old compost bags slit lengthways, stapled to the fence base and overlapped by 30cm (1ft), work well and last indefinitely.

More substantial barriers can be built from bricks, breeze blocks, slates or even old rubber conveyor belts. If installing a permanent barrier isn't feasible (say on an allotment), then a 60cm (2ft) deep perimeter trench will keep out most perennial weeds, but always keep it covered to avoid accidents. On an allotment, as well as sinking a vertical barrier into the soil, keeping a 30–45cm (12–18in) wide strip of ground around the perimeter of the plot permanently covered will stop all annual weeds, and deter weedy grasses such as couch (p.58) which may invade from paths around the plot. Use strips of black polythene or old natural-fibre carpet.

A dense evergreen carpet of (from front to back) sedum, heather (*Erica*) and variegated euonymus keep this drive edge weed-free

Using ground cover plants

Covering the ground with a dense permanent layer of attractive spreading plants is a highly effective way of 'designing out' weeds, and there are many different ground cover plants to choose from. Thorough ground preparation is essential before planting ground cover, which is highly effective when used in conjunction with synthetic mulches – see p.94.

Some flower and vegetable crops are also highly effective as temporary ground cover. The large leaves of pumpkins and squashes form a dense, shade-casting canopy over the ground, which stops weeds from germinating. Trailing Surfinia petunias, when grown as bedding plants, will smother the ground, producing a dense, colourful carpet of flowers and foliage.

A thick canopy of pumpkin leaves makes useful temporary ground cover in summer, elbowing out all but a few easily removed groundsel

Useful ground cover plants for an earth-friendly garden

The following are all suitable for permanent planting and have flowers that provide a source of food for bees and other insects. Some, such as *Rubus tricolor*, also have fruits that are eaten by birds.

Geranium maccrorhizum smothers weeds and provides spring forage for bees

Perennials:

Bistort (*Persicaria vacciniifolia*)

Bugle (*Ajuga reptans* 'Atropurpurea')

Catmint (*Nepeta x faassenii*)

Ceratostigma plumbaginoides

Dead nettle (*Lamium maculatum* 'Beacon Silver')

Elephant's ears (*Bergenia* spp.)

Golden marjoram (*Origanum vulgare* 'Aureum')

Hardy geranium (*Geranium macrorrhizum*)

Lambs' ears (*Stachys byzantina* – avoid non-flowering 'Silver Carpet')

Lungwort (*Pulmonaria* spp.)

Shrubs:

Ceanothus thyrsiflorus var. *repens*

Creeping thyme (*Thymus serpyllum*)

Erica x darleyensis 'White Perfection'

Hebe pinguifolia 'Pagei'

Herringbone cotoneaster (*Cotoneaster horizontalis*)

Prunus laurocerasus 'Otto Luyken'

Purple sage (*Salvia officinalis* 'Purpurascens')

Rose of Sharon (*Hypericum calycinum*)

Rosemary (*Rosmarinus officinalis* 'Prostratus' group)

Rubus tricolor

Green manures

These are excellent at preventing weeds, especially in the vegetable garden from autumn to spring. Green manures are plants that can either be incorporated into the soil to help boost fertility, or be cut down and left as a home-grown mulch on the surface, while their roots decompose and form humus in the soil. Some, such as field beans, are sown in autumn and act as a living mulch during the winter months. Their leaves cover the soil, preventing the germination of weed seeds, while their roots stop plant nutrients being washed away by winter rains. Green manures are ideal for a bed system in a kitchen garden, but can be used to great effect almost anywhere.

Using a bed system

Dividing your vegetable plot into a series of beds 90–120cm (3–4ft) wide with 45–60cm (18–24in) wide paths helps prevent weeds. The beds can either be flat on the ground or have their sides raised with wooden boards. The soil in the beds is usually cultivated at the outset, but then soil disturbance is kept to a minimum, so that few fresh weed seeds are brought to the surface. Nor are the beds trodden on, making it easier to remove any weeds from the uncompacted soil. Weeding one bed thoroughly is more of a morale-booster than having to tackle an entire weed-covered plot. The paths are kept weed-free using a mulch such as straw.

Beds are often kept covered with mulch (see 'Mulch magic', p.92) and any seeds, as well as young plants grown in modules (see 'The right start', p.86), are sown/planted by parting the mulch layer. Planting in blocks also helps to cover the soil and stops weeds from germinating – see 'Growing techniques to foil weeds', opposite.

A mulch of dead fern fronds prevent weeds and protect the soil in this bed from winter rains

Growing techniques to foil weeds

• Several weeks ahead of sowing or planting, rake an area level, removing hard soil clumps and large stones, then leave it. Within a matter of weeks (depending on the time of year), the ground will be covered in a flush of small weed seedlings. These can then be hoed off using a razor-sharp hoe, taking care to disturb only the very surface layer of the soil. You can now sow your seeds as normal. This technique (known as a 'stale seed-bed') exhausts the weed 'seed bank' at the soil surface resulting in far fewer weed seedlings to compete with crops.

• Seedling weeds can be hard to tell from germinating crops, making it difficult to weed crops when the plants are small. Give crops a head start by sowing into a seed drill as usual, then covering the seeds with a thin layer of old potting compost or fine leafmould. These will contain virtually no weed seeds so crops get off to a flying start and are then easy to tell apart from seedling weeds.

• Placing plants close together in blocks, rather than rows, so that they quickly form a canopy of leaves that shade the soil below, helps prevent weeds from germinating. This technique works well with large, leafy vegetables such as cabbages, bedding plants or even perennials.

• Growing crops in a different part of a kitchen garden each year – known as 'crop rotation' – will help prevent a build-up of weeds, especially annuals. Potatoes and other leafy crops, such as pumpkins and squash, form an excellent living mulch – their dense canopy of leaves stops light reaching weed seeds. Rotating these crops around the garden (or between beds) helps to avoid a build-up of specific types of weed.

Use water wisely

Weed seeds need moisture to germinate. During the summer you can drastically reduce weed germination by carefully 'spot watering' your plants. Rather than using a sprinkler, which wets a large area of soil, try directing the water to the base of individual plants, using either a push-button watering can or a trigger-operated lance attached to a hosepipe. I make a saucer-shaped depression around the base of plants as I plant them. This acts as a mini reservoir, allowing water to soak in around the roots, but leaving the surrounding soil dry.

Mulch magic

For me, using a mulch – mulching – lies at the very heart of earth-friendly weed control. It plays such a vital role in chemical-free weed prevention and control that I would encourage you to become a 'mulcher' at every opportunity. Mulching really can work 'magic' in the garden. It can mean the difference between hours of hard, ineffective and demoralising weeding, and a garden or allotment where weeds, when they do appear, can be dealt with quickly, easily and effectively.

A straw mulch stops weeds from germinating, breaks down into the soil and increases fertility

In the dark

A mulch is any material laid over the surface of the soil. This not only helps prevent weeds but keeps the soil below moist. The main reason mulching stops weeds is that it prevents sunlight reaching the soil surface, so weed seeds cannot germinate. No matter how many thousands of weed seeds are lying dormant in the soil, unless they receive light (plus moisture and warmth) they cannot spring into life. If you are taking over either a brand new garden or an established one with areas of bare soil, cover it up as quickly as possible, using straw, leaves, grass mowings, cardboard, black plastic, old carpets – anything that will block out the light. These might look unappealing, but removing them when you start developing your garden will be a lot easier than hacking your way through a wilderness of weeds.

Breaking down

Biodegradable organic mulches – straw for example – will break down into the soil, add plant nutrients and organic matter, and stimulate soil life, most noticeably the activities of earthworms. To be effective an organic mulch must be at least 5cm (2in) and preferably 8–10cm (3–4in) thick and cover the soil completely, with no gaps. As the mulch decomposes and is incorporated into the soil, it will need topping up, at least annually, to keep weeds at bay. Organic mulches are most effective on ground that has already been cleared of weeds, although a 10–15cm (4–6in) deep layer spread over young annual weeds will kill them, especially if they are hoed off first.

Although mulching will dramatically cut down on your workload, it won't solve all weed problems. Most perennial weeds can push their way through even a thick mulch, except when you use a tough, impervious material like black polythene. To eradicate tough weeds, be prepared to keep affected parts of your garden covered with a sheet mulch (see p.96) for several years and let nature do the hard work.

Synthetic mulches

There are several types of non-biodegradable, synthetic mulches available that don't decompose and will last for many years. Here, a woven plastic mulch, in sheet form, which is porous, allowing rain and air (but not light) to pass through it, is preventing weeds in a mixed border containing perennials and shrubs. The area was first cleared of all perennial weeds, garden compost/manure was incorporated (these can't be added after the mulch is laid), and the sheet was laid over the whole area. Planting was done through 'x'-shaped planting holes and then bark chips were spread in a 2.5cm (1in) deep layer to disguise the plastic sheet and protect it from the sun.

Some organic mulching materials, clockwise from top left: grass clippings; straw; well-rotted manure; cardboard; hay; bracken; newspaper; soft shredded prunings; feathers. These are often free, are biodegradable and will readily break down into the soil

Clearing weed-infested ground

In many gardens and allotments, preventing weeds is simply not an option; you must first deal with those already present. This is especially true where the garden or plot has been left untended to run wild for many months or even years. In these circumstances, getting rid of weeds can seem a daunting, if not impossible, task and there might seem to be hours, days and weeks of back-breaking hard work ahead. While some hard work is inevitable when you begin to clear ground of long-established weeds, if you think in 'bite-size chunks', divide the area up into manageable sections and use a sheet mulch on the worst areas, you will succeed.

Sheet mulching – the big cover-up

The technique of sheet mulching involves covering weed-infested ground with a thick, dense 'sheet' or layer made up of different types of mulching material, which starves both annual and most tough perennial weeds of light. Sheet mulches usually need at least a year or more to be effective, but you can easily plant through them and grow crops while the weeds below are still dying away. This technique can be used to clear any piece of ground, whatever its ultimate use. If ground is riddled with perennial weeds, leaving the mulch down for two to three years might be necessary to weaken and kill the most persistent of them, and their remnants might still need clearing out – see 'Forking and digging', p.101.

I cleared an overgrown allotment of weeds with sheet mulching, and began harvesting six months later

The major advantage of using a sheet mulch over other ways of clearing weed-infested ground is the saving in time and effort. From my own experience, I've estimated that to cover an average-sized allotment with sheet mulch should take you, once you've gathered together the materials, no more than a good day's steady work. To dig the same area would probably take you at least two weeks' hard work, with some digging every day and at weekends. Of course you don't have to clear the whole area at once; if your time and energy are limited, concentrate on a smaller area first, then move on to another.

After laying a sheet mulch, minimal weeding, occasional watering, and harvesting fresh food was the hardest work I had to do

Perhaps the biggest hurdle to overcome with sheet mulching is, surprisingly, a psychological one. To most minds, clearing a garden or allotment of weeds is synonymous with hard, back-breaking work. It simply seems impossible that a weedy plot can be transformed into fertile, productive ground without any digging or other soil cultivation, but it really does work. I once turned a weedy allotment into a productive food garden in less than six months and never used a spade to dig the soil once. The 'no-dig' approach (see p.100), where soil is rarely if ever turned over (which works well on a bed system – see p.90), is highly effective in preventing and controlling weeds.

Sheet mulching is probably the most potent, earth-friendly way of dealing with weed-infested ground I know, so give it a try.

How to lay a sheet mulch

This is my proven method of clearing weedy, reasonably level ground of all annual weeds and most perennials (it can be used just as effectively to turn a lawn into a food garden in a single season). Ideally, a sheet mulch should be laid in mid- to late spring, as the soil begins to warm up, so that weeds are starved of light just as they begin to grow. If the mulch is laid in winter, it will keep the soil cold during spring and any crops planted through it will struggle to grow. If you take over a plot in summer, cut down the weeds or fell them with a rotary line trimmer – they can be left on the surface to rot down into the soil. Tough woody weeds like bramble (p.54) should be dug out.

1 Clear the area of any large debris, then lay large, flat sheets of cardboard over the area to be cleared, overlapping them by 30cm (1ft) at the edges so that no light can pass through. Packaging for fridges and freezers

Large, overlapping sheets of cardboard are ideal for sheet mulching

The overlapped sheets are weighed down with a 10cm (4in) layer of compost or manure

is ideal and readily available. On smaller areas, opened-out full-thickness newspapers work just as well. If the ground is riddled with tough perennial weeds like great bindweed (p.63), you can use old natural-fibre (as opposed to rubber-backed) carpets, which break down slowly and are excellent as a long-term mulch.

2 Hold the cardboard in place with a layer of garden compost, rotted manure, good-quality topsoil, fallen leaves, lawn mowings, leafmould, soft shredded prunings – any organic material that has some weight to it. This layer doesn't need to be more than 10cm (4in) thick. If materials are in short supply, or if you are covering a large area, concentrate the material along the 'seams' where the sheets of cardboard overlap. Wads of fresh or spoiled straw/hay can also be used.

3 As a final touch, a 5cm (2in) layer of straw or hay can be laid over the top, to keep the sheet mulch looking neat and tidy and to retain moisture, although this isn't essential. If straw or hay are hard to obtain, ask your neighbours to donate their (weedkiller-free) lawn mowings and spread these over the sheet mulch as a final topping.

What happens next?

As the mulch settles, any weeds underneath are starved of sunlight, die and rot into the soil. The cardboard begins to crumble and decompose, and worms start to pull organic matter down into the soil, helping to improve its fertility. Dormant weed seeds at the surface don't germinate because there is no light. The shoots of perennial weeds like creeping thistle (p.59) and curled dock (p.59) will penetrate the mulch layer, but they are quite easy to remove, along with their roots, if the soil around them is loosened first. In a year's time, the ground will be clear of any annual weeds, and all but the most pernicious of perennial weeds, and will be covered with a light-excluding, weed-suppressing mulch. Areas where perennial weeds are hanging on will be obvious. Once the ground is cleared you can either adopt a no-dig approach, or you can cultivate the now weed-free soil, removing any remnants of perennial weeds at the same time.

No-dig gardening

The no-dig approach means earthworms do the 'digging'

Respect for the soil and the life within it is the essence of no-dig gardening. Apart from any initial cultivation, perhaps to remove troublesome weeds or relieve soil compaction, the soil is never turned over. Garden compost and other fertility-building or soil-improving materials, which usually have a dual role as a mulch, are spread over the soil surface but not incorporated by digging; this job is left to earthworms, which improve drainage and soil structure, while other soil organisms decompose further what the worms drag down, releasing plant nutrients and forming humus. Although some disturbance of the soil is inevitable when sowing, planting and harvesting, it is minimal compared with that caused by digging which, in the long term, is detrimental to most soils.

The benefits of no-dig gardening are:

- **Far fewer weed seeds reach the surface**
- **The hard work of digging is no longer required**
- **Soil life flourishes in the stable, undisturbed soil**
- **Losses of moisture and organic matter are reduced**
- **Over time, soil structure improves and remains intact**

Weeding a no-dig plot is usually easy. On bare soil, regular hoeing will gradually exhaust the seed bank near the surface, while other weed seeds remain buried and dormant in the soil. Organic mulches, like straw, will prevent any weeds from germinating and can be scraped apart to allow for sowing or planting. Any perennial weeds can be loosened with a fork, then lifted out, disturbing the soil as little as possible. Going no-dig makes perfect sense if you've used a sheet mulch (see p.98) to clear an area of weedy ground, and can play a vital role in helping keep a garden free of weeds.

Forking and digging

Lifting, turning and breaking up the soil to remove the underground parts of shallow-rooted perennials is the traditional way of clearing weed-infested ground. On a small area, or after a larger area has been cleared using a sheet mulch, forking or digging the soil can be highly effective. By loosening the soil and breaking it down into fine crumbs, it is possible to remove even the tiniest fragments of roots and rhizomes. Using a fork has the edge over a spade, which easily severs weeds (as well as worms) below ground, making it harder to trace them if the roots go down deep. Moist soil is far easier to dig or fork over.

Use a fork to loosen the soil around weeds with taproots, such as this dandelion

Bury them deep

Burying weeds starves them of light so that the leaves quickly turn yellow, die and decompose into the soil. For burying to be effective, the weeds must be buried at least 15cm (6in) deep. A word of caution: burial is not effective for most perennial weeds, especially those with spreading underground parts, and if you chop up and bury the taproots of weeds like dandelion (p.60), each piece can produce a whole new plant. Burial is most effective when you are single-digging ground that has become covered with a carpet of young annual weeds. As each spadeful of soil is turned over, the spade is used to slice off the weeds just below soil level. They will then fall into the trench and can be buried as digging proceeds.

Double-digging, where the soil is cultivated 'two spades deep' (to the depth of twice the blade of the spade), can be useful when removing deep-rooted perennial weeds, although some, such as field bindweed (p.62), send their roots much deeper than this and will still regrow. However, although double-digging won't eradicate such serious weeds, it will help weaken them.

Tread and bruise

Bracken (p.53) dislikes being trampled underfoot, so this can be an effective method of control. Tread the shoots flat in late spring and early summer when they are 15cm (6in) tall, leaving them attached to the plant rather than cutting them off. Repeat the trampling whenever new shoots reach that height – this exhausts the food stores in the tough underground rhizomes. You can also control bracken by regular cutting – see 'Chop, slash and trim', opposite.

Mowing out

One effective – if slightly extreme – way of dealing with troublesome perennial weeds is to grass down a weedy part of your garden using either turf or seed and treat it as a lawn. Both ground elder (p.64) and field horsetail (p.62) can be eradicated using this technique, although it could take two to three years to clear them completely. This clearance technique works because the weeds are weakened by having their leafy tops cut off each time the grass is mown. This needs to be done regularly.

Young buckwheat plants cast dense shade which suppresses weeds

Smothering

Being a densely-growing, leafy crop that quickly shades the soil, prevents many weed seeds from germinating and smothers most annual weeds and some perennials, potatoes are often used to help 'clear' new ground. Harvesting potatoes also helps to loosen hard, compacted soil, and you can remove any weed roots at the same time. You can grow potatoes anywhere in your garden to help clear the ground, even if the area is earmarked as an ornamental border.

Buckwheat, a green manure (see p.90), is another useful fast-growing smothering crop, which is sown in late spring on any cultivated areas that won't be needed for several months. It quickly chokes out all but the toughest perennial weeds, it sends nutrient-seeking roots (which are thought to release natural weed-suppressing chemicals) deep into the soil, and its flowers are a magnet for hoverflies, making it ideal for an organic garden. At the end of the season plants can be cut down and left as mulch on the soil surface, where they will help prevent weed seeds from germinating.

Chop, slash and trim

Chopping down actively growing weeds with a sickle or weed hook will certainly reduce them, but it will only be a temporary measure. The same is true of rotary line trimmers – they make a neat job of cutting weeds off at ground level, but perennials will soon shoot again. However, simply cutting down weeds can be effective if you don't have time to clear weedy ground, but need to stop them from flowering and producing seeds. Wear gloves and cover your skin when chopping your way through a weedy wilderness; the sap of some weeds, like great bindweed (p.63) and hogweed (p.67), can cause blistering, especially in hot sun.

Some weeds can be beaten by regular cutting. Cutting down bracken (p.53) two to three times starting in late spring, for two successive years, will help to eradicate it (the fronds make excellent compost or mulch); a similar approach can be taken with stinging nettle (p.78), which also makes great compost (see p.109).

Biological control

If you have a problem with couch grass (p.58), great bindweed (p.63) or ground elder (p.64), perhaps on the boundaries of your garden, natural 'biological' control is worth a try. *Tagetes minuta* or Mexican marigold is a 1.5m (5ft) tall half-hardy annual (and relative of French and African marigolds) which can be planted, after the last spring frosts, among colonies of these troublesome weeds. Chemical secretions from its roots are thought to suppress and weaken their growth. Raise *Tagetes minuta* under cover so it gets an early start.

Hoeing, hand weeding and flame weeding

Even a well-kept garden will have weeds from time to time. Recurring problems are more likely in regularly cultivated areas, such as the kitchen garden or borders used for growing bedding plants, where disturbing the soil brings weed seeds to the surface where they can germinate. Low-weed zones will be any parts of the garden that are covered with a mulch (see p.92), such as permanently planted mixed borders, or no-dig beds in the kitchen garden where soil disturbance is minimal.

The following methods of weed control are part of the day-to-day maintenance of your garden and are just as important as other jobs such as watering and feeding. They are included here, following on from weed prevention and clearance techniques, because they are ways of dealing with localised weed outbreaks once the more serious weed problems in your garden have been overcome.

Off with their heads – hoeing

A hoe is a sharp blade fixed to a handle, which is used to slice off seedling weeds, especially annuals, just below soil level. The decapitated seedlings then wilt and die, while the roots are unable to regrow. A Dutch or 'push' hoe, where the front edge of the blade does the cutting, is the easiest to use. For hoeing in between closely spaced plants, such as you might have on a bed system, or among bedding plants, an onion or 'swan-necked' hoe is ideal. In this

A Dutch hoe is used to control seedling and young weeds by cutting them off at the soil surface

case the blade is fixed at the end of a short, curved metal neck and weeds are cut off using a backward chopping action. There are many other types of hoe available – some are gimmicks – but a Dutch and/or onion hoe is ample for most situations.

Observing the 'golden rules' of hoeing will guarantee effective weed control:

- Keep the hoe blade sharp at all times.
- Hoe when it's sunny and breezy and the soil surface is pale and dry – don't hoe after rain or if the soil is dark and wet.
- Frequent, regular hoeing when weed seedlings are small is the most effective.
- The hoe blade should run parallel with the ground, just skimming the surface and cutting the weed seedlings off cleanly, just below soil level. Practice makes perfect.
- Take extra care when hoeing near crop plants or flowers, to avoid damage.
- Avoid hoeing perennial weeds like couch grass (p.58), which will regrow from fragments of chopped-up rhizome. Instead, loosen the soil with a fork and lift them out.
- Remember that hoeing will only cut off the tops of taprooted weeds like dandelion (p.60) temporarily – it won't kill them.

To be effective a Dutch hoe must be kept razor-sharp

Weeds with masses of fibrous, shallow roots are easy to pull up whole

This sun spurge has white sap, which can irritate skin, so wear gloves when weeding

Pull them up

The simplest way of removing weeds is to grab hold of them and uproot them. It's also the most earth-friendly way of weeding there is – just you versus the weed. This is quite easy with shallow, fibrous-rooted weeds like groundsel (p.65), but is almost impossible with deep, taprooted weeds such as curled dock (p.59). If a weed won't pull up easily, rather than tearing off the top and leaving the roots to regrow, use a fork to loosen the soil beneath it, then ease the whole weed out. You can also remove spreading but shallow-growing perennials like couch grass (p.58) this way.

Hand weeding is the most effective way of removing annual and young perennial weeds from in amongst garden plants, where using a hoe would cause damage. Take care when hand weeding along rows of young seedlings, pulling up only single or small groups of weeds at a time, to avoid disturbing the soil and uprooting your plants. A hand fork or trowel is extremely useful for loosening soil when removing weeds by hand.

Flame weeding

Sometimes called 'thermal' weeding, this technique is used to kill weeds when they are seedlings or in the very earliest stages of growth. It is most practical and effective on paths and drives with lots of crevices, and along the base of walls. In a flame gun,

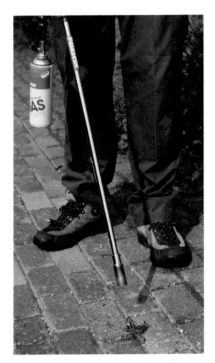
Flame weeders are useful for killing weeds in the cracks in paving

gas passes from a cylinder to the end of a tube, feeding a hot flame, which is passed just over the top of the weeds. Flame weeding works by 'boiling' the weeds – the flame only needs to lick the weeds until they turn either lighter or darker green, and wilt slightly. Afterwards they quickly shrivel, turn brown and die, although perennials may need repeat treatment. There is no need to blacken and incinerate the weeds, or to produce smoke.

A flame gun can also be used in the vegetable garden, to kill seedling weeds that germinate ahead of the crop you've sown. Timing is critical; you must flame the weeds before the crop seedlings emerge or they will also be killed.

Although this technique uses a 'fossil fuel' which releases carbon dioxide, it does not pollute the soil and/or water sources. Targeted, sparing use of a flame gun is a compromise between laborious hand weeding and the use of polluting chemical weedkillers.

How to finish off tough weeds

In any weeding session you can soon accumulate bucketfuls if not barrowfuls of weeds – a mixture of shoots, roots and some soil, which should be returned to the garden after composting. If your haul is mostly soft, sappy annual weeds, these can go straight into the compost bin or onto a heap, but chop them up with a spade first and leave them to wilt for a few hours. Perennial weeds, especially their tough roots, runners and rhizomes, are more of a problem because a new plant can grow from just a small fragment. Even in the dark of a compost bin, couch grass (p.58) can survive for many months and then reinfest your garden hidden among the compost.

Finishing off tough perennial weeds is actually quite simple, even though it may take a little longer. Using the following techniques there's no excuse for putting any weeds – a rich source of organic matter and plant nutrients – in your dustbin. By recycling every last bit of organic garden waste you are helping to reduce the huge amount of organic material going unnecessarily into landfill sites – a true waste of natural resources. If you must remove green waste from your garden, make sure it goes into special collection facilities, where it will be recycled by your local authority.

Wilt and weaken

Make a point of using a spade to chop up perennial weeds, then spread them out in the sun, preferably on a sun-baked path or even a shed roof. This won't kill the thick taproots of, for example, dandelion (p.60), but it will weaken them, especially if they are chopped up small. Another option is to put them through a shredder, or even pass over them with a rotary mower with its grass box fitted.

Letting weeds wilt in the sun reduces their bulk, making them easier to handle, and in the meantime they help to stop the soil drying out

Composting

All weeds can be composted. I don't have perfect compost bins or heaps that get hot enough to actually kill weed seeds, but instead make very sure that any weeds likely to cause me problems, usually the perennials, are as dead as they can be before I add them to my bins. If you want a hot bin or heap – it requires determination, time and effort to succeed – consult a book that explains the process in detail (see p.129). Apart from the problem perennials, all other weeds go straight in. Large clumpy ones are chopped up, and I always try to wilt everything first.

It's true that adding the flowers and seed-heads of weeds to your compost will mean dormant seeds travelling back to your soil in the resultant compost, but I rely on mulches (see p.92) to keep weed seeds dormant anyway. What I might lose by not having a 'hot' composting system that kills many weed seeds by 'cooking' them at high temperatures, I gain from using effective weed prevention measures – especially 'magical' mulches.

In the bag

To make your own weed bag, turn an old potting compost bag inside out, fill it with chopped and wilted perennial weeds, puncture some air holes all over it, then soak the contents in a solution of one part fresh urine to ten parts water. Nitrogen-rich urine helps kick-start the composting process by stimulating the breakdown of organic matter, but isn't essential. Seal the bag and put it in a sunny spot where, being black, it will heat up quickly, speeding the breakdown process. In a year's time the weeds will have become rich, dark compost.

Several months after being bagged up, these perennial weed roots are beginning to rot down

Drowning is a guaranteed way of finishing off even the worst perennial weeds

Drowning

Place your perennial weeds in a bucket (use a barrel for large quantities) then fill it with water and weight the weeds down with a brick. A few weeks later, starved of air, they will start to rot down and form a pungent slurry. The liquid can be poured out on to the garden and what's left added to your compost bin to complete the breakdown process. This is a foolproof way of disposing of any amount of even the most persistent weeds. A similar technique using stinging nettle (p.78) produces a valuable liquid plant food – see p.43.

Organic weedkillers

So-called organic weedkillers, usually based on vegetable fatty acids, work by burning off green plant growth and are most effective on annual weeds with soft, fleshy foliage and when used over a small area. Although they will destroy the leaves of perennial weeds, they don't affect the roots. They are biodegradable, but the spray could kill useful ground-living creatures, such as beetles, if they come into contact with it. An earth-friendly approach to weeds means there should be no need to use chemicals at all – even 'organic' ones.

Weeds in lawns

I shudder when I see young children playing on an apparently healthy, dark green, completely weed-free lawn, knowing that a few days before that same lawn was drenched in a potent mix of chemicals. Lawns containing weeds can be beautiful, tough, hardwearing and perfectly functional for most of our needs. In times of drought, some weeds – yarrow (p.80), for instance – stay green better than grasses, while black medick (p.52) survives in poor soils by accumulating nitrogen in its root nodules. It then slowly releases the nitrogen, feeding the grass. A carpet of daisies (p.60) in full flower is simply stunning and the flowers of bird's-foot trefoil (p.51), white clover (p.79) and self-heal (p.76) are a rich source of food for bees. Many lawns contain a wide range of wild plants – weeds – that help to support a surprising quantity of wildlife, all of which forms part of your garden's ecosystem.

You might be content to enjoy a lawn rich in biodiversity, in which case eliminating most weeds won't be a priority. But if certain troublesome weeds are ruining your lawn, or you'd simply like to tip the balance a little more in favour of grass, there are earth-friendly measures you can take.

Low-growing self-heal creeps among lawn grasses, producing pretty flowers in summer

Sheep's sorrel is easily identified by its arrowhead-shaped leaves

- Encouraging the grass to grow strongly is the top priority in tackling lawn weeds without resorting to chemical weedkillers. Leave the mowings on the lawn in late spring and summer to feed the grass and stimulate soil life, especially earthworms, and feed it regularly with an organic lawn food. Scarifying to remove thatch will encourage grass, as will spiking the lawn to aerate it and relieve compaction, especially on well-used areas.
- Avoid mowing the grass too short; close-mown and 'scalped' lawns tend to encourage weeds while taller grass will help to shade out, smother and weaken them. Set the cutting height on your mower no lower than 2.5cm (1in).
- Eliminate the causes of weed problems. Sheep's sorrel (p.76) thrives in acid soil, so raising the pH by liming (to raise the pH to 6.5–7.0) will deter it and also encourage earthworms. Creeping buttercup (p.58) favours damp conditions, so improve the drainage. Resow shady areas where grass is failing and weeds are thriving, using a shade-tolerant lawn seed mixture containing meadow grass.
- Physically remove problem weeds. The flat leafy rosettes of hoary plantain (p.66) and dandelion (p.60) can be lifted out by loosening the soil around them first with a fork, or you can use a weed 'grubber' or old kitchen knife to cut through the roots below soil level. Fill the holes left with a mixture of old potting compost and grass seed.

- Bare patches, caused by wear and tear or where annual meadow grass (p.51) is dying out, should be reseeded or turfed as soon as possible, to prevent any dormant or airborne weed seeds from germinating.
- Use a spring-tine rake to loosen and lift the stems of spreading weeds like black medick (p.52), so they stick up, then mow with the grass box fitted and wilt the mowings in hot sun before composting them.
- With a severely weed-infested lawn, replacing the turf – or at least the worst-affected areas of it – might be a drastic but more practical solution. This way you can completely eliminate most of the existing weeds and start from scratch using a grass seed mixture suited to your situation. Replacing a lawn is also an opportunity to remedy long-standing problems – such as compacted soil, poor drainage or low fertility – which may have encouraged the weed problems in the first place.
- Don't waste weedy turf stripped from a lawn; stack it upside down in a heap, soak it well, then cover it with black plastic or an old carpet. In a year's time it will have turned into rich, crumbly garden compost. An alternative to stripping off weedy turf is to lay a sheet mulch (see p.96), which will kill off all plant growth, including any grass. Once the ground is clear, the soil can be prepared as necessary and a new lawn sown or laid.
- If part of your lawn is already more weeds than grass, consider handing it back to nature and turning it into a 'bug bank' – see p.44.

Tackling moss

Moss thrives both on moist, poorly-drained soil and in dry, acid soil with poor fertility, especially in shade and where grass is cut very short. Improving drainage, raising the soil pH, feeding the grass regularly, letting it grow to 2.5cm (1in) tall and raking the moss out in spring and autumn will all help deter it. Reseed any bare patches after raking.

At-a-glance guide to preventing, clearing and controlling weeds in different garden situations, using an earth-friendly approach

Situation/problem	Method	See page
Introducing new plants	Check for weeds	86
Flower beds (bedding plants)	Hoeing	104
	Hand weeding	106
Perennial/shrub/ mixed borders	Mulching	92
	Hand weeding	106
	Hoeing	104
	Ground cover plants	88
Established kitchen garden	Use module-raised plants	86
	Use appropriate growing techniques	91
	Targeted watering	92
	Mulching	92
	Hoeing	104
	Hand weeding	106
	Burying	101
	Smothering	103
	Crop rotation	91
	Adopt a no-dig approach	100
	Flame weeding (seedling weeds)	106
Vegetable 'bed system'	Mulching	92
	Hand weeding	106
	Hoeing	104
	Green manures	90
	Crop rotation	91
	Adopt a no-dig approach	100
	Flame weeding (seedling weeds)	106
Established fruit garden	Mulching	92
	Hand weeding	106
	Adopt a no-dig approach	100

Seed-beds	Use appropriate growing techniques (inc. stale seed-bed)	91
	Flame weeding	106
Paths, drives, patios, gravel areas	Flame weeding	106
	Hand weeding	106
	Hoeing	104
	Grubbing out (cracks in paving)	112
Neglected, weedy ground	Sheet mulching	96
	Digging/forking out	101
	Cutting/slashing	103
Hedge bottoms	Digging/forking out	101
	Mulching	92
	Ground cover plants	88
	Biological control	103
Garden boundaries	Physical barrier	86
	Digging/forking	101
	Biological control	103
Containers	Hand weeding	106
	Mulching	92
Rockeries/scree	Hand weeding	106
	Mulching	92
Bases of young trees	Mulch/synthetic fabric	94
	Hand weeding	106
	Rotary line trimmer	103
	Ground cover plants	88
Brand new garden (bare, rough ground)	Mulching	92
	Sheet mulching	96
	Hoeing	104
	Digging/forking	101
Allotment (neglected/overgrown)	Sheet mulching	96
	Digging/forking	101
	Cutting/slashing	103

Under cover (greenhouse/ polytunnel/coldframe)	Digging/forking	101
	Hand weeding	106
	Mulching	92
	Hoeing	104
	Physical barrier	86
Weeds spreading from neighbouring garden or allotment	Physical barrier	86
Airborne weed seeds	Cutting/chopping down source before seeds released	103
	Physical barrier	86
Self-seeding garden plants	Hoeing	104
	Hand weeding	106
	Mulching	92
	Remove immature seed-heads	103
Persistent perennial weeds	Sheet mulching	96
	Digging/forking	101
	Mowing out	102
	Treading/bruising	102
	Frequent hoeing	104
	Biological control	103
Lawn	Various	111

Afterword

I'm constantly amazed at just how readily people douse their gardens in synthetic chemicals, be they insecticides, fungicides – or weedkillers. Perhaps even more amazing is the ease with which they then use treated areas of the garden for recreation, or even for growing food. On my allotments I've seen plots blanket-sprayed with weedkiller at various times, and then watched their owners harvesting produce from among the poisoned, dying weeds perhaps only a few weeks later.

The insidious use of weedkillers by local authorities is also a cause for concern; the brown, dead fringes bordering our streets, roads and footpaths is becoming an all too familiar sight. That much we can see. What isn't obvious is just where the several thousand tonnes of garden chemicals (including weedkillers) that we put onto our gardens each year finally end up, and exactly what the effects are on the world in which we live. Little is currently known about either the short- or the long-term effects of most garden chemicals, either on ourselves and the more obvious wildlife around us, or on all the life we can't see, especially in the soil.

Weeds clearly shows how it's perfectly possible to tackle weeds in any garden situation without resorting to a chemical quick fix. I believe that gardeners and their gardens, large or small, have a profound and vital role to play in healing some of the damage already done to our environment. Understanding, working with and, when necessary, tackling weeds in ways that are kind to the earth is a great start.

Dead, sprayed-off fringes are now common in public areas

Glossary

Airborne seeds: any weed seeds carried on and distributed by the wind.

Alkaline: soil with a pH above 7.0.

Allotment: an area of usually publicly owned ground rented out for growing plants, often food crops.

Annual weed: one which completes its life cycle in one year.

Apomixis: the ability of certain native wild plants to produce seeds without pollination or fertilisation taking place, e.g. dandelion (p.60).

Bed system: the practice of dividing an area, usually a vegetable garden, into a series of narrow beds that are worked from paths.

Bedding plant: any ornamental annual, biennial or perennial plant, raised almost to maturity in a pot, which is then planted or 'bedded out' in the garden for a temporary display.

Beneficial insects: any insects that have a positive effect in the garden, such as pollinating crops (e.g. bees) or reducing pest populations (e.g. hoverflies).

Biennial weed: one that takes two years to complete its life cycle.

Biodegradable: any substance that breaks down harmlessly, usually in the soil.

Biodiversity: the variety of plant and animal life found in a natural habitat, garden or specific part of a garden.

Biological activity: the combined activities of both large and small organisms in the soil, or in a compost bin/heap.

Biological control: the practice of using certain plants to suppress persistent perennial weeds.

Block planting: the practice of planting crops, usually vegetables, in blocks at regular spacings to form a dense canopy of leaves that will suppress weeds.

Botanical name: the name by which any weed (or plant) is known throughout the world.

Bug bank: a 'wild' area of a garden where certain weeds and garden plants are grown together to attract beneficial insects and other useful creatures.

Bulb: a swollen, usually perennial, food storage organ that produces leaves and flowers. Some bulbous weeds produce bulbils, which help them spread.

Burying: the practice of covering weeds, usually annuals, with soil while digging.

Capsule: the dry, seed-bearing structure produced by some weeds, which splits open when ripe.

Caterpillar: the larval stage of butterflies, moths and certain other insects.

Common name: any localised name by which a weed is known; weeds can have numerous common names but only one botanical name.

Companion weeds: those that are said to encourage and/or improve the growth of adjacent crops.

Compost bin/heap: any container filled with organic material or heap of stacked material, which then rots down to form garden compost.

Composting: the process of making garden compost using organic material gathered from the garden.

Creeping roots: those that spread below ground, sometimes over considerable distances.

Crop rotation: the practice of growing crops in a different part of the garden/bed each year.

Cultivated ground: soil that is used for growing crops, usually vegetables, and which is relatively weed-free.

Cutting down: reducing established weeds using a sickle, weed hook or rotary line trimmer.

Diseases: problems affecting plants caused by fungi, bacteria or viruses.

Dormant: weed seeds in the soil that have the potential to germinate when they are exposed to the right conditions.

Double-digging: cultivating the soil to twice the depth of the blade of a spade, or approximately 45–60cm (18–24in) deep.

Dutch hoe: a sharp blade attached to a long handle, which is used to hoe off weed seedlings with a forward pushing action.

Earth-friendly: any gardening activity that shows positive regard for, and works with, nature rather than against it, including preventing, clearing and controlling weeds without the use of chemical weedkillers.

Earthworms: soil-living invertebrates that help to incorporate organic matter and improve drainage, soil structure and aeration.

Ecology: the study of how living organisms relate to each other and their environment.

Edible weeds: any weeds that can be eaten, raw or cooked.

Environment: the natural surroundings in which people, animals and plants live.

Ephemeral weed: one that completes its life cycle rapidly and is able to produce several successive generations within a year.

Explosive pod: a seed pod that explodes and scatters seeds over a wide area.

Fertilisation: the joining of male and female sex cells following pollination of a flower.

Fibrous roots: a mass of thin roots, which are usually easy to pull up by hand.

Flame weeding: using a flame gun to control seedling weeds.

Flower bed: any place where bedding plants are grown, usually for a temporary summer display.

Forking: using a garden fork to loosen soil and remove weed roots, often perennials.

Frond: the divided, compound 'leaf' of bracken (p.53) and other ferns.

Fungal disease: a plant disease caused by a fungal pathogen.

Fungicide: a substance used for controlling fungal diseases.

Garden compost: decomposed organic matter that is dark and crumbly when it is removed from a compost bin/heap.

Garden ecosystem: the community of living organisms in your garden, including weeds.

Garden plant: any plant that is deliberately grown in a garden.

Grass down: turn an area into lawn using turf or grass seed.

Green manure: a thick-growing crop used to cover otherwise bare soil, suppress weeds, stop leaching of plant nutrients and increase soil fertility.

Greenhouse effect: the warming of Earth's atmosphere due to release of carbon dioxide and other 'greenhouse gases', some of which are released during manufacture of garden chemicals, including weedkillers.

Ground cover plant: any ornamental plant with a low, spreading, dense habit that covers the ground and helps to prevent weeds.

Grub out: remove weeds from lawns or between cracks in paving using an old kitchen knife or a 'grubber'.

Half-hardy: any plant that is unable to survive frost – i.e. temperatures below 0˚C (32˚F).

Hand fork: a small, hand-held fork with short tines, used for loosening soil and helping to remove weeds by hand.

Hand weeding: removing weeds by hand, such as by pulling them up.

Hardy: any plant that can survive outdoors all year round – i.e. temperatures below 0˚C (32˚F).

Hibernation: a torpid state adopted by animals, insects and other creatures during the winter.

Hoeing: using a hoe to control seedling and young, usually annual, weeds.

Hoverfly: a fast-moving, often striped insect whose larvae feed on aphids.

Humus: a dark brown substance found in the soil resulting from the natural decomposition of organic matter.

Indicator weeds: those that give clues to the fertility, pH or drainage of a soil.

Insecticide: a substance used for killing insects.

Leafmould: a fine, dark and crumbly material resulting from the breakdown of leaves.

Life cycle: the way in which weeds grow and reproduce, and over what timescale.

Liquid feed: any liquid containing water and plant nutrients, which boosts growth and/or improves plant health.

Liverwort: a flat green plant often found on the compost in pot-grown plants.

Manure: a mixture of animal faeces, urine and straw, which should be allowed to decompose before use in the garden.

Medicinal: any weed having therapeutic properties.

Mixed border: a border where perennials, bulbs, shrubs and sometimes trees are grown together.

Module tray: a tray with individual cells, in each of which a single plant is grown so that it develops its own root system. This allows transplanting with minimal disturbance to the roots.

Mowing: cutting a lawn using a lawnmower.

Mowing out: the practice of grassing weedy areas down, then mowing them regularly to weaken and clear certain perennial weeds.

Mulch: any biodegradable or non-biodegradable material spread over the soil surface, which blocks out the light, prevents weed seeds from germinating and conserves moisture. Some organic biodegradable mulches help increase soil fertility.

Natural fatty acids: materials of vegetable origin that remove the waxy coating from weeds, thereby killing them. Found in some 'organic' weedkillers.

Natural habitat: where wild creatures are naturally found.

Nettle bank: a colony of stinging nettles (p.78) grown deliberately in a garden.

No-dig: the practice of leaving soil undisturbed, apart from initial cultivation, and then allowing earthworms to incorporate organic matter, which is spread over the surface.

Node: the point on a stem, sometimes swollen, where leaves, buds, shoots and roots arise.

Nutrients: minerals necessary for healthy plant growth and development.

Onion hoe: a small, hand-held hoe with a curved neck, which is useful for hoeing between plants.

Organic approach: a philosophy and approach to gardening which shows positive regard for nature, working with and alongside it, rather than against it.

Organic matter: any once-living material that is used to improve soil fertility and/or is suitable for mulching.

Overwintering: the ability of some weeds to survive the winter without being killed by frost.

Peat-free compost: a specially formulated potting mixture which does not contain peat. Extraction from peat bogs causes environmental damage and habitat destruction.

Perennial weed: one that survives indefinitely from year to year.

Perimeter trench: a deep trench dug around the edge of an allotment to help prevent invasion by spreading perennial weeds.

Permaculture: the harmonious integration of landscape and people to provide their food, energy, shelter and other material needs in a sustainable way, that works with, rather than against, nature.

Pernicious weed: any particularly aggressive weed with a tendency to spread, that resists attempts to eradicate it.

Pesticides: substances, often synthetic chemicals, used to kill insects or other animals which can damage plants.

Pests: organisms, most commonly insects, which feed on plants and cause damage.

pH: the measure of the acidity or alkalinity of the soil, measured on a scale of 0–14.

Physical barrier: any impenetrable material sunk into the ground to prevent the lateral spread of perennial weeds through/over the soil.

Pinnate: a compound leaf with individual leaflets arranged on either side of the leaf stalk, often in pairs opposite each other.

Pioneer weeds: the first weeds to appear on recently disturbed ground, usually annuals.

Plant nutrients: those nutrients, such as nitrogen (N), phosphate (P) and potash (K), which are essential for plant growth.

Pollination: the transfer of pollen from one flower to another.

Potting compost: a specially formulated mixture containing plant nutrients, which is used to grow plants in containers. Peat-free composts are preferable in an earth-friendly garden.

Pulling up: physically removing weeds by hand.

Raised beds: garden beds where the sides of the bed are raised up, generally using wood.

Reseeding: scattering lawn grass seed on to bare patches in lawns.

Rhizome: an underground stem that can produce roots and shoots at its joints (nodes).

Root: the below-ground part of a plant responsible for absorbing water and plant nutrients and providing anchorage.

Root nodules: small pale nodules found on the roots of weeds such as white clover (p.79) which contain nitrogen-fixing bacteria.

Rosette: a flat, circular arrangement of leaves at soil level.

Rotary line trimmer: a device with a thin cord spinning at high speed that cuts through plant growth. Often called a 'strimmer'.

Rotary mower: A lawn mower that cuts grass using a flat, rotating, horizontal blade.

Runner: a stem that runs out over the surface of the ground, then roots at its nodes where it touches the soil.

Sap: the liquid that oozes from broken weed leaves, stems and roots and may blister and/or irritate skin.

Scarifying: removing 'thatch' from a lawn with a spring-tine rake or a powered scarifier.

Seed drill: A straight groove made in finely-raked soil into which seeds are sown.

Seed pod: the part of a weed containing seeds, which develops as the flowers fade.

Seedling weed: Any weed when it has just germinated and produced its seedling leaves (cotyledons).

Self-fertilisation: the ability of a weed to fertilise its flowers with its own pollen and to produce viable seeds without the need for another plant.

Self-seeding/self-sown: any plant's ability to perpetuate and spread by scattering its own seeds as soon as they are ripe.

Sheet mulch: A thick, dense, light-excluding sheet or layer of various materials which kills annual and many perennial weeds, and is used to clear badly weed-infested ground.

Shredded prunings: any tough or woody (but non-thorny) prunings or stems that have been passed through a shredder and are useful as a mulch.

Shredder: a powered machine that can be used to chop up tough perennial weeds to help weaken them before composting.

Shrub: a plant with a permanent woody framework of branches above ground.

Sickle: a small, hand-held, crescent-shaped blade used for cutting down weeds.

Single-digging: turning over the top 15–30cm (6–12in) of topsoil using a spade.

Smothering: preventing and/or controlling weeds using dense crops such as potatoes.

Soil fertility: a measure of the amount of available plant nutrients found in soil. These are essential for plant growth, and boosting soil fertility generally results in better crops.

Soil structure: the arrangement of soil particles into larger units; well-structured soils tend to have a loose, crumbly consistency.

Spiking: making holes in a lawn to improve drainage and aeration.

Spot watering: applying water to individual plants around their base.

Spring-tine rake: a rake with long, sprung tines (teeth) used to remove moss and thatch from a lawn, and to lift lawn weeds prior to mowing them off.

Stale seed-bed: a technique used to exhaust the 'bank' of weed seeds found at the soil surface, ahead of sowing crops.

Stolon: a long, often arching stem that roots at its tip when it touches the soil.

Subsoil: the layer of less fertile, sometimes paler soil found immediately below the darker, more fertile topsoil.

Synthetic chemicals: any chemicals used in the garden derived from an artificial process, such as weedkillers. These are unsuitable for an earth-friendly garden.

Synthetic mulch: any mulching material that is artificial and non-biodegradable and doesn't break down into the soil.

Taproot: a thick, vertical root reaching deep into the ground and characteristic of some perennial weeds.

Topsoil: the top 15–30cm (6–12in) or so of soil that contains the greatest concentration of plant roots, humus, plant nutrients and biological activity.

Transplant: any young plant put into a permanent position where it grows on to maturity.

Treading: a way of weakening bracken (p.53), a perennial weed.

Trowel: a small, hand-held tool with a blade, used for planting and for loosening weeds.

Virus disease: a plant disease caused by a virus, which can be found in weeds and may also affect garden plants.

Weed: any plant growing where you don't want it, which competes with garden plants and/or interferes with gardening activities.

Weed hook: a tool with a curved, semi-circular blade used for cutting down weeds.

Weed-suppressing: any material or plant with properties that restrain weeds.

Weeding: removing weeds, by hand or using appropriate tools where necessary.

Weedkiller: a substance, usually a synthetic chemical, that kills weeds.

Wildflower: any native (or introduced) plant growing in its natural habitat, away from gardens or other cultivated places.

Wildlife: any non-domestic, naturally-occurring organisms.

Woody: having tough, fibrous stems that persist year-round.

Sources of useful information about weeds

Books about weeds

Allan, Mea, *The Gardener's Book of Weeds*, Macdonald and Janes, 1978, ISBN-13 0670756575 (out of print and covers weedkillers, but still well worth tracking down)

Readman, Jo, *Controlling Weeds Without Using Chemicals*, Search Press Ltd, 2000, ISBN-13 0855329341 (out of print)

Roth, Sally, *Weeds: Friend or Foe?*, Carroll & Brown Publishers Ltd, 2002, ISBN-10 190325826X (out of print)

Salisbury, Sir Edward, *Weeds and Aliens*, The New Naturalists Online, 2009, ISBN-13 9780007308286 (a detailed, fascinating study of weeds)

Identifying weeds

Blamey, Marjorie, Fitter, Alastair and Fitter, Richard, *Wild Flowers of Britain and Ireland*, Bloomsbury Natural History, 2013 (2nd edition), ISBN-13 9781408179505

Chancellor, R J, *The Identification of Weed Seedlings of Farm and Garden*, Blackwell Scientific Publications, 1983, ISBN-13 9780632007707 (out of print but useful for identifying seedling garden weeds)

Phillips, Roger, *Wild Flowers of Britain*, Pan, 1977, ISBN-13 0330251839 (out of print but an essential photographic guide)

Williams, John B, Morrison, John R, *A Colour Atlas of Weed Seedlings*, CRC Press, 2003 (2nd edition), ISBN-13 9781840760385 (colour photographs of 40 common weed seedlings)

Eating weeds

Fern, Ken, *Plants for a Future: Edible and Useful Plants for a Healthier World*, Permanent Publications, 2011 (2nd edition), ISBN-13 9781856230117

Mabey, Richard, *Flora Britannica*, Chatto & Windus/Sinclair Stevenson, 1997, ISBN-13 1856193771 (packed with information on common names of weeds, folklore and uses)

Mabey, Richard, *Food for Free*, Collins, 2012 (new edition), ISBN-13 9780007183036 (the classic work on edible wild plants, including many weeds)

Phillips, Roger, *Wild Food: A Complete Guide for Foragers*, Macmillan, 2014, ISBN-13 9781447249962

Mulching and no-dig gardening

Dowding, Charles, *Organic Gardening the Natural No-dig Way*, Green Books, 2013 (3rd edition), ISBN-13 9780857840899

Lanza, Patricia, *Lasagne Gardening*, Rodale Press, 1999, ISBN-13 9780875969626 (an American book, but packed with sound information on sheet mulching and no-dig techniques)

Pears, Pauline, *Growing Fruit and Vegetables on a Bed System the Organic Way*, Search Press Ltd, 2004, ISBN-13 9781844480128 (out of print)

Making garden compost

Foster, Clare, *Compost*, Mitchell Beazley, 2014 (revised edition), ISBN-13 978-1845338954

Pears, Pauline, *The Organic Book of Compost*, IMM Lifestyle, 2011, ISBN-13 9781847734372

Shepherd, Allan, *The Little Book of Compost: Recipes for a Healthy Garden and a Happy Planet*, Collins, 2007, ISBN-13 9780007267279

General organic gardening (with useful sections on weeds)

Caplan, Basil (ed.), *The Complete Manual of Organic Gardening*, Headline Book Publishing, 1994 (new edition), ISBN-13 9780747278306 (out of print but worth searching for)

Hamilton, Geoff, *Organic Gardening*, Dorling Kinderseley, 2011, ISBN-13 9780756671792

Pears, Pauline (ed.), *Garden Organic Encyclopedia of Organic Gardening*, Dorling Kindersley, 2008, ISBN-13 9781405334433 (out of print but a comprehensive guide to organic gardening)

Pears, Pauline and Stickland, Sue, *Organic Gardening*, Mitchell Beazley, 1999, ISBN-13 18400015857 (out of print)

Shepherd, Allan, *The Organic Garden: Green and Easy*, Collins, 2009, ISBN-13 978 0007290918

Stickland, Sue, *The Small Ecological Garden*, Search Press Ltd, 2006 (new edition), ISBN-13 9781844481552

Walker, John, *How to Create an Eco Garden: The Practical Guide to Greener, Planet-friendly Gardening*, Aquamarine, 2011, ISBN-13 9781903141892

Out-of-print titles can often be found by searching internet booksellers.

Gardening books with an earth-friendly emphasis are available from:

Eco-logic Books,
Mulberry House,
19 Maple Grove,
Bath BA2 3AF,
England.
Tel: 01225 484472.
www.eco-logicbooks.com
@ecologicbooks

Green Books,
UIT Cambridge Ltd,
PO Box 145,
Cambridge CB4 1GQ,
England.
www.greenbooks.co.uk
@Green_Books

Green Shopping,
The Sustainability Centre,
Droxford Road,
East Meon GU32 1HR,
England. Tel: 01730 823311.
www.green-shopping.co.uk
@Green_Shopping

Other sources of information

Garden Organic,
Ryton Gardens,
Wolston Lane,
Coventry CV8 3LG,
England.
Tel: 024 7630 3517
www.gardenorganic.org.uk
@gardenorganicuk

The UK membership organisation offering organic gardening
advice and information.

Index

Page numbers in **bold** refer to the main descriptive entry and photograph in 'Know your weeds' beginning on page 49.

About the author

John Walker is an award-winning gardening and environmental author, writer, blogger and micro-publisher with 40 years' experience in practical gardening, teaching and the garden media. He grew up in the countryside, caught the gardening bug while still at school, and then studied at the Birmingham Botanical Gardens, Cambridge University Botanic Garden, and the Royal Botanic Gardens Kew, England, where he was awarded the Kew Diploma in Horticulture. He is also a qualified horticultural teacher. John was features/deputy editor of *Garden Answers* magazine, contributing editor of *Kitchen Garden* magazine, and technical editor of *The Organic Way*.

John writes about greener, earth-friendly gardening for national newspapers and magazines, including *The Telegraph* and the Royal Horticultural Society's journal *The Garden*. His latest books, exploring gardening's place in nature, is the *Digging Deep in the Garden* series (see p.140). His book *How to Create an Eco Garden: The Practical Guide to Greener, Planet-friendly Gardening*, was shortlisted for the Garden Media Guild Practical Book of the Year in 2012. He wrote *The Bed and Border Planner*, was editor of *A Gardeners' Guide to Annuals*, and contributed to the *Garden Organic Encyclopedia of Organic Gardening*. John has won the Garden Media Guild Environmental Award three times, and has been shortlisted for Gardening Journalist of the Year three times.

John is currently making an earth-friendly garden at his home on the edge of woodland in Snowdonia, North Wales, where he is working with nature – including weeds – to help shrink his 'gardening footprint'.

Visit John's website www.earthfriendlygardener.net, follow him on Twitter at @earthFgardener, or send him an email at john@earthfriendlygardener.net

Author's acknowledgements

Warm thanks are due to the following: Erica Hunningher, who created the opportunity for this book to happen; Colin Leftley, who rises to any challenge with his camera; Anna Corbett for making many useful suggestions, and for challenging perceived wisdom; Pauline Pears of HDRA (now Garden Organic) and Jane Lawler of pbi for information on organic weedkillers; Joy Larkcom for the loan of several useful books and for advice on finishing touches; Ivy Salt for allowing photography at Corner Farm; East Staffordshire Borough Council for allowing photography in Stapenhill Cemetery, Burton upon Trent; gardeners of Bearwood Hill Road Allotments, Burton upon Trent, for providing some wonderful weeds to photograph; to my parents, who made the first edition possible; and to Richard Ellis, for believing this new edition was possible.

Did you enjoy *Weeds* and find it useful?

Without reviews from readers like you, it's hard to spread the word about independently published books like this one, and help them reach more readers. Just think: every person who reads *Weeds* might mean one less container of weedkiller being bought...

Leaving an honest review in the online store where you bought the book will only take a few minutes and it doesn't have to be long or complicated; just a few sentences sharing with other gardeners what you liked about *Weeds*, and what they might like about it themselves, is incredibly valuable to me.

In truth, very few readers leave book reviews. Adding yours will help me, as an independent, self-publishing writer, to sell more earth-friendly gardening books – and to create new ones.

Thank you.

Also by John Walker, published by Earth-friendly Books

Diverse, thought-provoking and cage-rattling collections of essays exploring gardening's place in nature.

Digging Deep in the Garden: Book One
ISBN 978-0-9932683-3-5

"John Walker is asking the sort of questions you don't usually find asked in gardening magazines."

Digging Deep in the Garden: Book Two
ISBN 978-0-9932683-5-9

"An intelligent reminder of the joys and responsibilities of gardening."

Available from:

- www.earthfriendlygardener.net
- Your local bookshop (by placing an order, quoting the book's title and ISBN)
- Online bookstores